Y0-BXW-733

A BEGINNER'S GUIDE TO Canadian HUMOUR

A BEGINNER'S GUIDE TO Canadian HUMOUR

Edited by
Lynette Stokes and Pamela Chichinskas
with contributions from
Nicholas Pashley   Larry Tyson   Anthony Jenkins

Eden Press
Montréal

A BEGINNER'S GUIDE TO CANADIAN HUMOUR
Edited by Lynette Stokes and Pamela Chichinskas

ISBN: 0-920792-73-1

© 1986 Eden Press
First Edition. All rights reserved.
No part of this book may be reproduced, stored in a retrieval system, or transmitted in any form or by any means, electronic, mechanical, photocopying, recording, or otherwise, without the written permission of the publisher.

Cover design: EDDESIGN
Cover Illustration: Anthony Jenkins
Inside Page Design: Lynette Stokes and Pamela Chichinskas
Photographs on pages 36, 44, 97 by Peter Lowery; page 37 by Luba Zagurak; pages 40 (bottom), 41 (bottom), 42, 43, 99 and 100 (top) by Fawn Duchaine; pages 39 and 43 (top) by Kendall Lougheed; pages 40 (top), 113 (bottom), 98 and 100 (bottom) by Patrick Johnson; page 43 (bottom) by Rodney Brent. All other photos from the private collection of Marmaduke Bott. Every reasonable effort has been made to trace ownership of copyright materials. Information that will enable the publisher to rectify errors or to include proper credit in future printings will be welcome.
Models appearing in photographs: page 127, Sharon Thompson as Princess Diawatha; page 119, Louis Boulay as Paul Schaffer.
The Publishers wish to thank Tommy and Starr Crawshaw for their ideas and encouragement.

Printed in Canada at Metropole Litho Inc.
Dépôt légal — quatrième trimestre 1986
Bibliothèque nationale du Québec

Eden Press
4626 St. Catherine Street West
Montreal, Quebec H3Z 1S3

Canadian Cataloguing in Publication Data

Main entry under titles:
    A Beginner's guide to Canadian humour

ISBN 0-920792-73-1

1. Canada--Anecdotes, facetiae, satire, etc.
2. Canadian wit and humor (English)   3. Canadian wit and humor, Pictorial.   I. Stokes, Lynette
II. Chichinskas, Pamela

PN6178.C3B44 1986   971'.002'07   C86-090214-5

Credits

Ukrainian Immigrant cartoon by Larry Tyson

Joe Clark cartoon by Anthony Jenkins

HOW BORING ARE WE? Conceived and written by Nicholas Pashley, Illustrated by Larry Tyson

THE CRASHING BORES OF CANADA Conceived and written by Nicholas Pashley, Illustrated by Larry Tyson

STANLEY KNOWLES' DIARY by Anthony Jenkins

VISIT THE SASKATCHEWAN WHEAT POOL Conceived by Lynette Stokes and Pamela Chichinskas, Illustrated by Larry Tyson

CANADIAN HUMOUR: A RETROSPECTIVE by Nicholas Pashley

DOMINION BOOKCLUB by Lynette Stokes and Pamela Chichinskas

ANOTHER DAY IN THE LIFE OF CANADA by Lynette Stokes and Pamela Chichinskas

FAMOUS CANADIANS' FAVOURITE COCKTAILS by Lynette Stokes and Pamela Chichinskas

DALHOUSIE DOC Conceived by Lynette Stokes and Pamela Chichinskas, Illustrated by Larry Tyson

FAMOUS CANADIAN EJACULATIONS by Anthony Jenkins

THE SOCRED ZONE Conceived and written by Lynette Stokes and Pamela Chichinskas (with thanks to Thomas Crawshaw), Illustrated by Larry Tyson

I, TRUDEAU by Lynette Stokes and Pamela Chichinskas

THE POETRY AND PASSION OF RALPH McRALPH by Anthony Jenkins

THE P.E.I. FUN PAGE by Anthony Jenkins

BAY STREET DICK Conceived by Lynette Stokes and Pamela Chichinskas, Written by Nicholas Pashley, Illustrated by Anthony Jenkins

SATURDAY LITE MAGAZINE by Lynette Stokes and Pamela Chichinskas

WORST CHOICE SUPER CHANNEL by Lynette Stokes and Pamela Chichinskas

'ALLO, 'ALLO POLICE Conceived by Lynette Stokes and Pamela Chichinskas, Illustrated by Larry Tyson

COLE PORTER'S ODE TO CANADA by Nicholas Pashley

Introduction

Nationalism without humour is like a cause without the célèbre. And yet, unlike most other countries who take their national identities too seriously, Canadians find grandiose displays of loyalty highly embarrassing. In fact, Canadians find almost everything highly embarrassing. Even Canadian Tire catalogues are delivered in plain brown wrappers!

So what *is* it that makes Canadians laugh? A **Beginner's Guide** road crew, cleverly disguised as ordinary Canadians, travelled from coast to coast in search of the answers. Their findings are published here for the first time.

This is a handy guide for those just beginning to dabble in Canadian humour; the highs and lows, the facts, the figures, and the lies. **Beginner's Guide** gives you the *real* dirt on the fastest, loudest, hottest nation in the first world. **Beginner's Guide** is the perfect book for an imperfect people.

PAGE THIRTEEN HAS BEEN CANCELLED DUE TO POPULAR SUPERSTITION

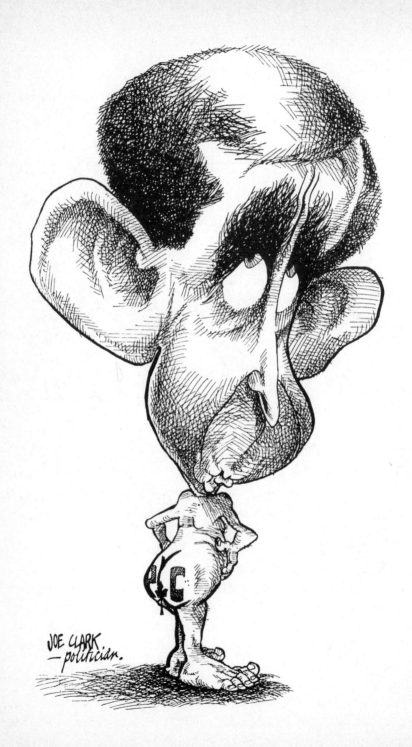

JOE CLARK
— politician.

LE CANADA · D'ABORD

How Boring Are We?

It is a misconception to assume that Canada is universally regarded as the most boring nation on earth. Certainly, all the surveys put us in the top ten. Well, all right, the top five. So have it your way, the top three.

A mere two decades ago, Canada was lucky to make it into the top twenty most boring nations in the world. We trailed behind perennial international bores like New Zealand, Belgium, Belize, and the Spanish Sahara. This was not through any lack of boringness on our part. On the contrary, it was our very national tedium that led to our lowly status in the international snooze stats.

In short, we were too dull by half. No one knew we were here. In the last two decades, however, we have come a long way.

Bit by bit we have crept past Oman, Ecuador, and Romania in international perception, until finally we are on the brink of big league boredom. Indeed, aficionados of national dullness have recently argued that we may now be the match of any nation.

It is merely official recognition that we lack at this point. Previous great bores have marred their high standings in recent years. Allegations of genocide in the seventies and eighties have, for better or worse, made Argentina and Chile respectively more interesting in the public eye. Massive starvation took Ethiopia out of the ho-hum stakes, perhaps for years to come. The Philippines needed only three or four months to drop out as a leading contender, Grenada did it in less than forty-eight hours, and it is difficult for us now to believe that once we ranked Iran and Afghanistan highly in the Sominex Stakes.

In the meantime, while we have done nothing here in Canada to impair our progress toward the top, it will clearly be difficult for us to dislodge the annual leaders. While we may have gained the bronze medal for international boredom, only a natural disaster (or another Canadian general election) could propel us into one of the top two places.

Switzerland, of course, is untouchable in first place. A stranger to tidal waves or earthquakes, Switzerland seems destined to hang on indefinitely to the crown they first claimed in 1658, the year they crept past Denmark on the strength of the mildly interesting Siege of Copenhagen. In all respects the Swiss have it. The spectacular nature of the countryside merely serves to accentuate the resolute, even dogged, tediousness of the Swiss. By comparison, Swedes are outgoing and jolly, a nation of stand-up comics. There is some doubt that the Swiss even invented the cuckoo clock.

A controversial choice for second place in international boredom is Japan. There are those who will argue *ad nauseam* in the defence of rich Japanese culture, art, history, etc. Let them. The Japanese are a nation of people who live to work, who will take a day off only if coerced by legislation. The Japanese are a people whose sole national preoccupation lies in trying to produce an ever smaller television screen. The only chance of catching the Japanese, it must be said, rests in that nation's taste for authoritarian governments or their unfortunate *penchant* for the earthquake. Either weakness could render the Japanese suddenly interesting and vault Canada into second place.

Canada's gradual climb into third spot has come as a result of steady boredom, rather than as a result of any significant single act of tedium. True, generations of hard slogging threatened to go by the boards in the early seventies while Prime Minister Pierre Trudeau was dating Barbra Streisand, but as time passed only the occasional inexplicable pirouette disturbed the still waters under which Canada rested. In recent years, the Joe Clark interregnum, the constitutional debate, and the rise of Brian Mulroney quietly and effectively carried Canada past Suriname, Equitorial Guinea, and the Marshall Islands into the top three, where, let it be said, we belonged all along.

For some reason, our neighbour to the south remains out of the top several spots. Money and power are unquestionably factors in this curious omission, though any nation that brings us Jim and Tammy Bakker, Ed McMahon, Senator Jesse Helms, Barry Manilow, the NFL, a tariff on shakes and shingles, the Statue of Liberty celebrations, Madonna, and the return of Bobby Ewing need take a back seat to no one when it comes to boring.

So what do they think of us out there in the rest of the world? Do they even know we're here? You bet they do. Talk to the man on the street in England (or Portugal or Greece or Jamaica or Hungary or Hong Kong or Italy or damn near anywhere in the world). He'll tell you: Canada? Sure, I know Canada. Cousin of mine went there to live. Very cold, he said. Will that do? That's all I know. The mike still on?

The CRASHING BORES OF CANADA

The Toronto Bore:

It's incredible what's happened to this town, you know, they don't call it Hogtown anymore, I mean you can get anything you want in Toronto now, there's every kind of restaurant you want, dim sum, tapas, sushi, you name it, we're incredibly cosmopolitan, you can get Heineken, Budweiser, and about a dozen different light beers, and what a movie centre, they made Middle Age Crazy here and Kane and Abel, *you get a lot of big names coming*

here, Mariel *Hemingway was here recently* *and Kris* *Kristofferson making a mini-* *series, I* *once saw Robert Vaughan on* *Yonge* *Street, all these people love it* *here it's* *very clean, hell,* *it's a world-* *class city now, and* *when we* *get the domed* *stadium* *it'll be great they* *say it'll* *bring in millions of dollars and really put us on the map, and now we're trying for the 1996 Olympics, that'll make the world sit up and take notice . . .*

The Weather Bore:

Well, the point is it's not so much the heat as the humidity, it's the same with winter, when I grew up on the prairies, sure it got cold, forty, fifty below, but it was a dry cold, you didn't feel it, but you take Toronto, it's a damp cold, it goes right through you, as I was saying back home on the prairies it could be sixty, seventy below and you could go out in a t-shirt, it was that dry you didn't feel it, of course I'm talking Fahrenheit, but of course at forty below it's all the same, Fahrenheit and Celsius, you may not have known that, which reminds me of the winter of '72, by the way do you know the formula

for figuring out the wind chill factor . . . . ?

The Bore Abroad:

No, well, actually since you mention it, there are plenty of well-known Canadians, Anne Murray for instance, and Paul Anka, Joni Mitchell, let's see, Neil Young, and whatsisname Leonard Cohen a friend of mine actually saw Leonard Cohen in a bar in Montreal at least he was pretty sure it was Leonard Cohen, then there's people like Lorne Greene, I don't know did you ever get Bonanza over here, and Art Linkletter, he was born in Saskatchewan I think, not many people realize that, well he was a guy on American TV a few years ago, "Kids Say the Darndest Things," no well maybe you never saw him here, but how about Kate Reid or Donald Sutherland or Christopher Plummer, he played Captain von Whosit in The Sound of Music with Julie Andrews, no she's English I know that, and there's Dan Halldorson the golfer who won the something-or-other Open a year or two ago or he nearly won it I can't remember which, come to think of it I think he shot 78 on the last day, and what about Wayne Gretzky the hockey player, a sort of modern Rocket Richard, well I can't believe you've never heard of Rocket Richard, and then there's Mary Pickford, you know even when she was quite old before she died she still remembered she was Canadian and did you know it was a Canadian who killed John Belushi . . .?

The Immigration Bore:

The point I'm trying to make is if someone comes to this country willing to work and make something of himself then fair enough, but you look at these people, half of them can't speak the language, they have no qualifications for anything and they just go straight on claim to be refugees but who knows, I mean I haven't even heard of half these countries they say they come from, and what about jobs, I mean with unemployment what it is it's ridiculous, you go into a variety store any time of night or day and who's working there but orientals, twelve, fourteen hours a day, well who can compete with that, and they're driving around in flashy cars, and have you seen the way they drive

The Returning Star Bore:

God, but seriously it's beautiful to be back home, I mean seriously this is my home no kidding, I can't imagine not living in Canada this is where I'm from for God's sake I always intend to keep a home here, Donald and I always try to get back here for Christmas, you can't call it Christmas in LA, really let's be honest, unfortunately the last couple of Christmases I've been on location, it's hell but let's face it that's the nature of the business, but seriously I'd love to work more in Canada, I'd love to do more theatre right here, but right now the work's in LA I intend to work here more but nobody asks me I guess they just assume I'm too busy haha, you know it's always been something of a dream to play Ophelia at Stratford you know you make a name as a comic but you want to do something more

substantial you tried to capture *know more serious, I've that side of me in my film work particularly in my most recent film* Getta Load of Those Tits, *what it's really about is an average woman who finds himself at a beach resort questioning what she's done with her life sure you have to put the girls in bikinis in it, you've got to sell seats, but it's anything but another teen sex comedy if you really look at what it's about*

The Alberta Bore:

Look, you compare the price of gas with what the price of gas should be, you can see that central Canada's getting an incredible deal but it's always been the same old story, Ontario getting a free ride on the backs of westerners, and you read the Globe and Mail it's always the same thing, easterners complaining about this and that, making fun of Don Getty and painting us all as rich right-wing cowboys, hell you take Edmonton it's got theatre and restaurants and all of that now not to mention West Edmonton Mall, a friend of mine just got laid off last week it's the same right through the whole oil industry but people in Toronto are driving around in their little Jap cars paying nothing for their gas, I'm not a separatist but . . .

The VancouverBore:

There's no place like it, I really mean it, look I can be skiing up at Whistler in the morning and in like twenty minutes if the traffic's okay I can be on my boat once I did it in sixteen minutes, I tell you it's God's country out here, I know a place out near Horseshoe Bay you can find magic mushrooms, not that I've actually done it myself, especially when we get a fair bit of rain which I guess we've had lately usually this time of year's just perfect, you should have been here a week or two ago I was out in the boat every day, of course the eastern press make it sound like it always rains here and we're crazy but let's face it they should talk, they're all so uptight in the east, there's no way I'd ever go back to Toronto I've been here two years now . . . .

The Montréal Bore:

Seriously, I hate to see what's happened to this city, you can't even call it Eaton's anymore just Eaton, it's as bad as Nazi Germany with this Bill 101, seriously you speak English downtown you might as well be wearing a yellow star, I blame the politicians for stirring it all up when I was young French-Canadians were happy to speak English, honest to God, and you tell me they're happier now than they were then, come on you try to tell me that, well you can't can you, and then they wonder why the big corporations move to Toronto, for two cents I'd go there myself, a friend of mine runs a store in Outremont and he had to change his sign it makes you sick, I'd go to Toronto in a shot they say you can get decent smoked meat if you know where to look, but I'd miss hockey . . .

Stanley Knowles' Diary

MARCH
S M T W T F S
1
2 3 4 5 6 7 8
9 10 11 12 13 14
16 17 18 19 20 21 22
23 24 25 26 27 28
30 31
BROWNLINE

8.00
9.00 *Sat in Commons*
10.00
11.00 *Went Home*
12.00

MARCH
S M T W T F S
1
2 3 4 5 6 7 8
9 10 11 12 13 14 15
16 17 18 19 20 21 22
23 24 25 26 27 28 29
30 31
BROWNLINE

Thursday
13
March

8.00
9.00 *Sat in Commons*
10.00
11.00 *Went Home*
12.00

MARCH
S M T W T F S
1
2 3 4 5 6 7 8
9 10 11 12 13 14 15
16 17 18 19 20 21 22
23 24 25 26 27 28 29
30 31
BROWNLINE

Tuesday
11
March

8.00 *Sat in Commons*
9.00 *Went Home*

MARCH
S M T W T F S
1
2 3 4 5 6 7 8
9 10 11 12 13 14 15
16 17 18 19 20 21 22
23 24 25 26 27 28 29
30 31
BROWNLINE

Friday
14
March

in Commons
Went Home

MARCH
S M T W T F S
1
2 3 4 5 6 7 8
9 10 11 12 13 14
16 17 18 19 20 21 22
23 24 25 26 27 28 29
30 31
BROWNLINE

Wednesday
12
March

8.00
9.00
10.00 *Sat in Commons*
11.00
12.00 *Went Home*
1.00
2.00
3.00
4.00
5.00

1986

MARCH
T F S
5 6 7 8
12 13 14 15
19 20 21 22
26 27 28 29
NLINE

Sunday
16
March

Went to Church
Went Home

MARCH
S M T W T F S
1
2 3 4 5 6 7 8
9 10 11 12 13 14 15
16 17 18 19 20 21 22
23 24 25 26 27 28 29
30 31

Saturday
15
March

Read
Hansard

294

295

73

71

75

6075

290

298

Canadian Humour
A Retrospective

It is not clear when Canadian humour began. Our native peoples are blessed with an ability to laugh, but little has been handed down to us from pre-European days. There is a story that the name Canada comes from a misunderstanding of Portuguese explorers who, when asked where this place was, answered, "Que nada!", or "Nothing here!" This may be the first recorded Canadian joke, although many Canadians regard the story as apocryphal.

After this auspicious beginning, Canada entered a fallow period. Frankly, this fallow period lasted a very long time. There are those who claim that it hasn't ended. All right, we haven't produced a Don Rickles or a Benny Hill, but no country's perfect.

It might be argued that Canadian humour really began with Stephen Leacock. You remember Stephen Leacock, the guy who wrote the piece about the guy going into the bank to open an account. There are still people who read Leacock, although today he is largely remembered in Canada through an annual literary prize awarded to the author of what is judged to be the least funny book published in Canada (in the unlikely event of this book being nominated, the publishers reserve the right to retract the previous statement).

After Leacock's death in 1944, Canadian humour entered another quiet period awaiting the arrival some time in the early fifties of those giants of Canadian entertainment, Wayne and Shuster. To any Canadian of a certain age, the words, "I told him, Julie, don't go!" are guaranteed laugh provokers. It is interesting that the only words from a Wayne and Shuster sketch that anyone can still remember were spoken by neither Wayne nor Shuster. Still, these guys were big. These guys played the Ed Sullivan show, like Elvis Presley, Topo Gigio, and Senôr Wences. And they're still around, every bit as funny in the eighties as they were in the fifties. Shuster's the tall one, doesn't make a lot of noise. He's not the funny one. Wayne's the short one, very noisy, lots of wacky faces. He's not the funny one either.

Since the golden age of Canadian humour — roughly that decade between the first appearance of Wayne and Shuster on the Ed Sullivan show and the revelations in 1966 of the Gerda Munsinger scandal in Ottawa — the genre has been reduced to jokes about hosers. "G'day, eh?" does not really represent an awful lot of progress from "Que nada!" True, we have produced a number of funny people and exported them by the dozen to Los Angeles, but it's unlikely any of their avocado-swilling, hot-tub-dwelling neighbours perceive them as Canadians, except that they persist in going to Los Angeles Kings' hockey games. Try to explain this authentic Canadian joke to somebody in Topanga Canyon:

"My uncle lives in Manitoba."
"Flin Flon?"
"Nope. Churchill."

Where this country really found its own unique voice, of course, was the Newfie joke. The Newfie joke came into its own in the early sixties, and cynics have dismissed it as merely a copy of the Polish or Irish joke. This is clearly absurd (well, all right, it isn't really, but indulge me). The highest form of the Newfie joke is the one about the two guys from Toronto who go on a fishing holiday in Newfoundland. Oh, you haven't? Well, all right.

It seems these two guys from Toronto go to Newfoundland for a fishing holiday. They hire a local guide, and for the first week everything's fine. Halfway through the second week, however, they start to get a bit bored. The weather turns grim, the fish stop biting, and there's nothing else to do. So they're out there, cold and wet, bobbing about in this leaky little boat, when one of the guys from Toronto feels something on his line. Well he hauls it in (this part can be drawn out for dramatic effect), and what does he see hanging from his hook but an old lamp. Needless to say, he has a look at this old lamp, shines it up a bit, and out pops this genie.

"Whooo-eee!" says the genie, "but that water's cold! Thanks, guys, I owe you one. How about three wishes? That's traditional."

"Sure!" say the three guys in the boat. "Alright!"

So the genie looks at the guy who had got him out of the water. "What about you? You got a wish?"

The guy from Toronto thinks a bit and says, "Well, you know, I've had a good holiday and everything, but right about now I'd like to be warm and dry back home in my Don Mills townhouse, watching the Blue Jays on TV with a case of good Ontario beer in the cooler."

"Okay," says the genie, snaps his fingers, and the guy vanishes. "And how about you?" the genie says to the other guy from Toronto.

The other guy from Toronto thinks and says, "Well, my buddy's got a good point there. I don't think this weather's ever going to clear up, and to tell the truth I'm getting a bit sick of fish, and I do believe there's an Argo game on the TV tonight after the Blue Jays game and I'd dearly like to be back in my condo in Mississauga with my favourite brand of light beer."

"No sweat," replies the genie, and the second guy from Toronto disappears, leaving just the local guy in his leaky little boat. "Okay, fella," says the genie to the Newfoundlander, "what's it to be?"

The Newfoundlander has a bit of trouble making a wish. Does he want a new boat, or for the price of screech to go down, or fish to go up? And he's a bit sad about being left alone. He didn't mind the weather, and he liked the guys from Toronto. They paid him well, and they told him all about Toronto and their jobs in advertising and all of it, and he misses them.

"Gee," says the Newfoundlander, "I wish those guys from Toronto were back here."

DOMINION BOOKCLUB

Featuring These Canadian Bestsellers

The Tarot Mutiny
by Robertson Davies

Carl Jung, thinly disguised as a bisexual juggler and oboe repair man, quits the circus to write his memoirs — but wonders whether it has all just happened in his mind.

Fearless Symmetry
by Northrop Frye

Frye asserts that, if we look carefully, most things can be broken down into groups that resemble each other. Virtually all of them are God. Those that are not, are green vegetables.

Je Me Souviens ... Mais De Quoi?
by René Levèsque

Quebec's deposed monarch and bad boy strains to recall his years in power. He explains how political pressures forced his retirement. "I was overtired as a skunk," he confesses.

The Condo Dwellers
by Margaret Laurence

A middle-aged writer remembers back to her first ten or twelve lurid sexual experiences with multi-racial amputees, and she wonders where she went wrong.

The Boringside Person
by Peter Gzowski

Yet another self-portrait by this tedious Torontonian who thinks that the rest of the country is interested in a further hundred anecdotes about CBC Radio.

The Housewife's Tale
by Margaret Atwood

Set in the futuristic community of Etobicoke, Offramp, a persecuted housewife, protests her victimization by overeating and abstaining from meaningful relationships.

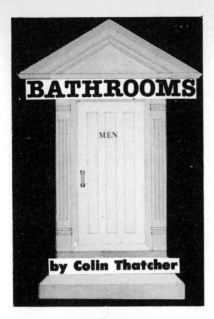

Bathrooms
by Colin Thatcher

Finally, in this no-holes barred account, Saskatchewan's best known politician and family man opens the doors to the provincial bathrooms. He tells what it's *really* like to live in Canada's most unforgiving province. "They're damn short of amenities, for a start," claims Thatcher. "It's a jungle out here."

The Spike Trilogy
by Pierre Berton

At last, Berton's famous trilogy is available in one volume. **The Next to the Last Spike, Only One Spike Left**, and **Just One Last Spike for the Road** tell the dramatic story of hundreds of sweating, beery men abnormally interested in spikes. A *must* read for the lobotomized.

* *Available in scratch and sniff editions.*

REDUCED TO CLEAR

CONDENSED EDITIONS

THE POCKET BRITANNICA..........$5.95
128 Information-packed Pages

ALL OR NOTHING....................$2.95
Winnipeg Jets Stanley Cup Highlights

WHO'S WHO IN NEW BRUNSWICK$3.95
Richard Hatfield Speaks Out

A MOVEABLE SNACK................$2.95
Ernie Hemingway's sizzling biography of Colonel Sanders

COUPON

YES! Send me this month's selection!

NAME _____

ADDRESS _____

✂ _____

PROVINCE _____

 GUARANTEE

If you are not completely satisfied with your choice, you may return it — collect — to: Senate Committee on Free Trade Talks Washington DC 20010

Another Day in the Life of CANADA

Photo: Peter Lowery

The publication of *A Day in the Life of Canada* inspired roving Beginner's Guide photographers to record for posterity the only remaining undocumented images of Canada. These shots were withheld from the original publication because of their controversial nature.

Stiff legislation has been enacted to stop dogs from defecating in Quebec lakes. Because of the extent of the pollution, an enraged populace has demanded that all dogs be refused defecation rights in the province. A treaty is being negotiated with the state of New York as a trade-off for their acid rain. The dog issue is now on the negotiating table.

Once famous as the Golden Square Mile, Westmount is no longer the bastion of rich, conservative anglophones that it once was. Despite attempts to suppress them, isolated outbreaks of *joie de vivre* have recently escalated into full-scale "festivals." The photograph below was passed clandestinely to Beginner's Guide by renegade anglophones.

Crasto, the up-and-coming Toronto performance artist, has recently received international acclaim for his pink multimedia extravaganzas. We see him here pinkwashing the inner compound of the Art Gallery of Ontario. Bravo Crasto!

Pitt Meadows, B.C., is fast catching up with Toronto as Canada's cultural mecca. The Heritage Society has spared no expense in maintaining their prestigious showcase museum. Beginner's Guide was given permission to photograph their latest thought-provoking exhibit.

Beginner's Guide has received
(from an anonymous source)
photos which reveal plans for
the expansion of the West Edmonton Mall. The Mall's
management, concerned that
Edmontonions no longer
live in the real world, felt
obligated to provide an
urban blight experience.

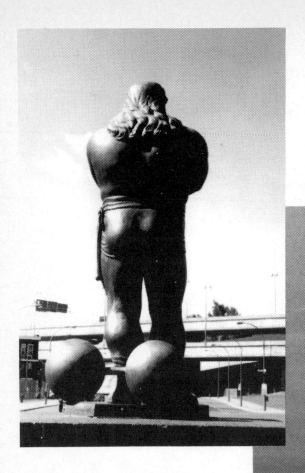

Well-known strong man and athlete, Louis Cyr (1863-1912) has long been a folk legend in Quebec.

The above photo is a rear view of the marble statue erected in Cyr's memory. The ghost of Cyr has been rumoured to hover over Lake St. Louis, assuming the same pose as the sculpture. Witnesses to these sightings are reticent to come forward, although one witness was persuaded to loan Beginner's Guide a photograph recording this astonishing event.

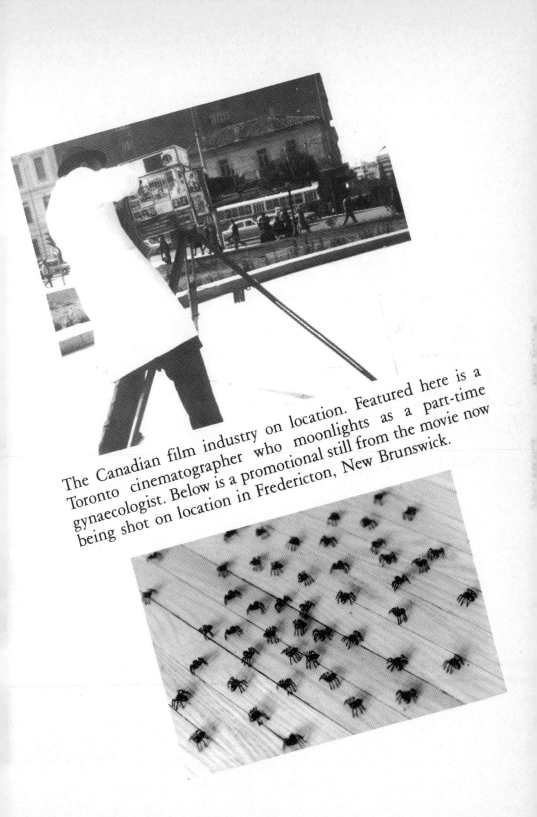

The Canadian film industry on location. Featured here is a Toronto cinematographer who moonlights as a part-time gynaecologist. Below is a promotional still from the movie now being shot on location in Fredericton, New Brunswick.

Vancouver's latest craze — vehicle art — started small, but people have subsequently gone to extreme lengths to prove that the medium is the message.

Famous Canadians' Favourite Cocktails

Bored? Sober? Tired of the same old YUPPIE drinks? Want to try something new? Beginner's Guide has made a cross-country survey of bartenders to the famous, and, as a public service, can now provide you with a list of famous Canadians' favourite cocktails.

But before you embark on your cocktail-making career, you should remember these handy tips: Cocktails are usually served before meals, but the following recipes are good at any time. Most famous Canadians prefer their drinks strong — more spirit, less flavour. You can adjust the potency to suit yourself or other drinkers.

The Gzombie

26 oz rum
26 oz vodka
26 oz gin
juice of one grape
stir, and serve in a
chilled bucket

The Moshartov
Cocktail

26 oz champagne
shake, and pour
into a glass
rimmed with
cocaine

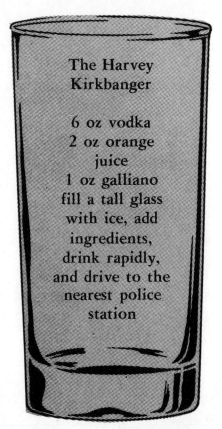

The Harvey
Kirkbanger

6 oz vodka
2 oz orange
juice
1 oz galliano
fill a tall glass
with ice, add
ingredients,
drink rapidly,
and drive to the
nearest police
station

The Bloody
Mila

1 bottle Dom
Perignon
pour into a
crystal cham-
pagne glass, sip,
and list as a
bona fide
business expense

The Margarita
Trudeau
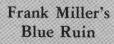
2 oz tequila
1 tbsp lime juice
1 dose triple sex
shake, rattle, and
roll

Frank Miller's
Blue Ruin

2 oz blue curaçao
1 tsp Pernod
2 oz vodka
blend and serve
to Conservatives

Famous Canadian Ejaculations

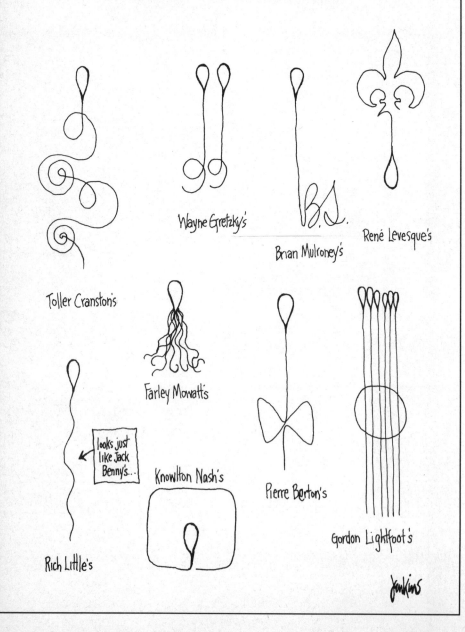

Submitted for your approval: Bill and Charlene Smith were recently married. Charlene was a teacher in Montreal until she was given her walking papers by her school board. Bill was laid off also from his job with a computer firm. Both were victims of departmental cutbacks.

The Smiths decided to go west in search of jobs, better weather, and the possibility of a better life. So, they loaded up a U-haul and drove west along the Trans-Canada.

As they near their destination they stop briefly, to reflect upon their arduous journey and the promise of this new land. Then, they cross the provincial boundary. Bill and Charlene have just crossed over into

THE SCORED ZONE

Beyond space, beyond time lies another dimension
British Columbia

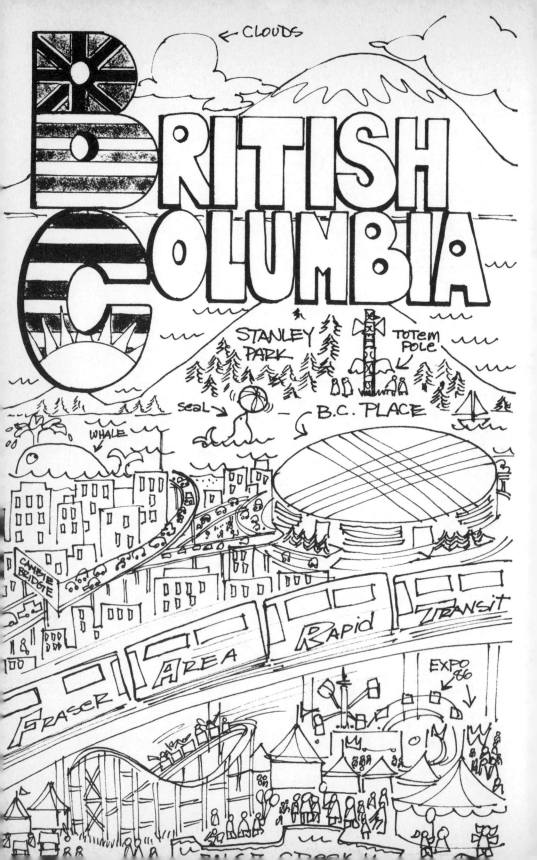

I, Trudeau

Chapter 1

The Days of Wine and Roses.

I, Pierre Elliott Trudeau, statesman, orator, playboy, lover, and intellectual, am about to write the inspired history of my life, in which I will recapture the folly and grandeur that once was mezzo-imperial Ottawa. There are those who have called me mad, drunk with power — lusting for control over others — but they do me an injustice. They are fools, and, if I had my own way, they would be hanged. But I digress.

In the beginning there was me. I was the word. And the word was conscientious objector. I did not approve of wars, thinking it more manly to sit astride a huge and throbbing motorcycle, doing and saying as I pleased, travelling from place to place, terrorizing harmless people in the street. It was but a small logical step from here to the House of Commons.

And yet, somehow, I felt at home in Ottawa. I was glad to be out of Québec, away from the jurisdiction of the monster Duplessis and his Union Nationale. Quiet revolution was not my style, and I bided my time under the wing of the weak but well-meaning Lester Pearson. Although Pearson was afraid to give me anything greater than mere justice minister, I knew that I was destined for greater things. I would bring brilliance and charisma to Canadian politics. There would be a new epoch — the Trudeau Era. I would be their God, and they would turn and look my way and grow pale. I would give the historians something to scribble about.

Time passed. No-one remembers the petty issues of the early sixties — at least not until Pearson saw his future in the stars and resigned from office, one of the mortals of Canadian politics. What followed was a convention of sorts, after which I was made leader of the Liberal Party. It was a dull affair, as I recall, by which I set little store. I wore a blue suit, I believe. And I was neither surprised nor impressed when colleagues burst into my private sauna to announce that I had been elected Prime Minister of Canada. At last, the universe was unfolding as it should.

And so I went out to my public, slipping a scarlet rose into my buttonhole. How proud it must feel! And, as the crowd gathered underneath my hotel window, I felt inspired. Throwing aside the French windows (throwing aside things French was soon to be an eccentricity of mine) I confronted the multitudes. Oh what I could have done with loaves and fishes now! "Viva Castro," I called to them. And there followed a stunned silence. Only the sound of screaming teenagers, and the haunting melody of Burton Cummings and the Guess Who crooning "These Eyes," could break the spell.

But, as with all things in politics, the magic was short-lived. It was 1970, and the Québecers were bored. They had come to my realization — and who doesn't eventually? — that a quiet revolution was no revolution at all. So, strange francophone youths roamed the streets looking for action, abusing political figures, and grabbing headlines from coast to coast. Well, I would deal with their arrogance. I would crush these provincial upstarts. October Crisis! Ha! I have had bouts of constipation that have troubled me more.

And yet no sooner had I dealt with this irritation, than I was dealt two bitter blows. The first was a foolish marriage, but that I could deal with. Far worse was my betrayal by a fickle and depraved electorate after I had enjoyed only four short years in power. I went to the polls and was insulted by a piddling two-seat lead in the Commons. Did I really have to depend on the whims of the shallow upstart, David Lewis, who had already been poisoned against me.

But worse storm clouds were gathering. I had committed hubris by equalling the Gods in beauty, power and character, and they sent René Lévèsque against me. At first I thought I could crush him with a glance, but what followed was such an alcoholocaust that I suspect neither of us can exactly remember the details. It was not long before certain members of my own party saw the opportunity for treason, and plots against me began to be hatched from within my own sanctum. Chief amongst these was the neurotic and megalomaniac Turner, who I banished from my sight as punishment.

Never has natural genius been so much misunderstood. I was born modest, and yet have been accused of overweening vanity. My jaunty wave to the good folk at Salmon Arm in British Columbia was misconstrued, and I was continually subjected to insulting fuddle-duddle on the floor of the house. So I became tired of the silly game. I had had enough of John Turner and his intrigues against me. He had left the arena, but had all this time been plotting for my overthrow. I would walk away — let them see if they could manage without me. But what of my legacy? Chrétien would be my heir. He was my champion and I sent him into the ring against them. How devastated I was to find that he had been given only the job of head waiter! I was well-punished for my trifling faults and eccentricities.

But now, as I sit quietly in retirement in the confines of my small, private, walled garden, I can see five burly men in white coats edging towards me. Ha! I see Duplessis . . . Turner . . . Lévèsque . . . do they think I can't see through their disguises . . .

The Poetry & Passion of Ralph McRalph

Ralph McRalph is one of Canada's national resources like lumber, wheat or hockey players. Unheralded, even in his native Cape Breton, McRalph's poetry is a passionate cry from the heart of things Canadian that speaks to us all. This is the first published retrospective of his work.

Hope

My UIC's run out,
So's my wife,
And the cat's developed a nasty cough.
Still, Spring's around the corner,
And that's something, eh?
1968

Lament

You can get 'Bud' in New Brunswick now,
The King of Beers they call it.
The Queen is on our money,
Last time I had some.
1985

Did you hear about the Torontonian who returned from an autumn vacation in Prince Edward Island with his face bandaged? Seems he happened upon a game of 'Bobbing for Fries' and insisted on going first.

Q. What's rich, brown and best without eyes?
A. Stevie Wonder or a P.E.I. Grade A Potato.

WHO'S DIFFERENT ?

One of the four 'Happy Taters' below is slightly different. Can you pick him out?

Darken the areas with a 'dot' in them to reveal favourite toppings for french fries.

Answers: vinegar, salt, ketchup, mashed potatoes.

1.   2.   3.   4.

Answer: #3 (He's from New Brunswick!)

BAY STREET DICK

I was sitting in my office downing the first spritzer of the day and reading the paper when the intercom buzzed. "Gentleman to see you," Sonia sang through the box, her voice like the northbound train coming into the King Street Station behind schedule.

I winced. "Tell him I'm out," I growled. The kind of year Dave Stieb was having at the ballyard had left me in no mood for chat.

"He says it's important," Sonia purred, sounding like Friday night traffic on the Don Valley Parkway as heard from the 34th floor of a Windy Golfway condo.

"Of course it's important," I snapped back. "It's always important. Everything I do is important." I was overreacting, I'll admit. I was as testy as an untipped waiter in a Yorkville bistro. "Tell him I'm out of town. Tell him I'm on a case. Tell him I'm at my fitness class."

I went back to the paper. Eurydice, 19, enjoyed wind surfing, rock music, and literary criticism. Her dream was to play Hamlet. She had a frame like a proscenium stage. No kidding, she was built like a Haliburton outhouse. I skipped through the paper. My biodex was down. Way down. That explained plenty. I'd been feeling as low as a Queen Street East taproom.

"Excuse me, sir." It was Sonia again. Listening to Sonia was like standing next to the Wild Mouse at the CNE. I got worried. I always get worried when Sonia calls me sir. We've been through plenty together, Sonia and me. She's indispensable. Sonia can book a squash court with her eyes closed and both hands tied behind her back. I've seen her do it.

"In the name of all that was wrong with city planning in this town prior to 1972," I sputtered, "what is it?" Sometimes Sonia's logic was as difficult to follow as the Rosedale bus route. I was mad. I was as mad as a motorist caught in a speed trap on that clear stretch of Yonge Street between St. Clair and Davisville.

"This guy insists on talking to you, sir," came the voice like a Macdonald-Cartier Freeway road crew. Now I was plenty worried. Worried and confused. I was as bewildered as the Leaf management. That was two sirs now. I didn't get it. Nobody was

better at getting rid of somebody than Sonia. She was tougher than an El Mocambo bouncer, and only half the size. Before I could say another word, she broke in again, her voice like a skate blade sharpener.

"He's offered me a better job, sir," she said. "Another ten K a year with a parking space and a profit-sharing scheme."

Holy Mimico, I thought, this guy's playing hardball.

"And there's a women's softball team," she went on like the canned laughter in a Wayne and Shuster special. "They play every Wednesday night, with free drinks afterwards at Pat and Mario's."

I whistled softly to myself and did some quick calculations. This guy was big league. First class and very big league. "You'd better show him in," I said, feeling as down as a sacked Argo quarterback. Tell the truth, I was feeling like a thirsty man outside an Ontario Liquor Board store five minutes past six on a Saturday evening. I was feeling like the guy who gets to Honest Ed's two minutes too late for the gate-crasher specials. I was feeling — well, you probably get the picture. I wasn't feeling good, put it that way. If you want to know, I'd been out pretty late the night before, throwing back spritzers at the Bellair Cafe. I'd been out till midnight, maybe later, and I wasn't at my best. Good thing I'd quit smoking anyway, or I'd have had a throat like the Bay Street underpass south of Front Street.

The guy who walked in just then was someone I'd never seen before. He was as unfamiliar to me as Thornhill. But something about the man said money. His suit was telling me big bucks. I mean, big bucks wholesale on Spadina even, but this guy was not Spadina. This guy was Bay Street, nothing less. But then, so was I. I don't know what my suit was saying. I spoke first, as usual.

"Sit down, Mr. —"

"Let's leave names out of it," he said.

"Fine with me," I replied, cool as Section 22 at the ballpark when the wind's coming in off the Lake. In my business, a lot of people don't want to talk names. That's jake with me. If I want to look at a bunch of names, I can read the phone book.

"I hear you're the best," he said. He had a quiet, smooth voice, like the air conditioning in my '84 Bonneville.

"You won't get an argument from me," I said, nonchalant as Borje Salming picking up the puck behind his net. Like the big Swede, I knew I was capable of an end-to-end rush if I felt like it. Accelerate like hell, leave a couple of guys standing still at centre ice, unload a big slapshot at the blue line, and watch the red light flash on — that was my style too.

"Good," the stranger said. "I need the best." The tone of his voice, cool and subtle like the cheese tray at Winston's, told me he could afford the best.

"I need you for something big," he said. "Something really big."

I pricked up my ears at this. I was on the case like Tony Fernandez on a ground ball. I was all ears. The way this guy said "real big," it sounded like very, very big. Everything about this guy said very big. The man was substantial. He was built like an old Chevy, without the fins. Still, I was cool. I was as casual as a junior partner at a Tory, Tory, Deslauriers, Binnington staff picnic, i.e., casual but very attentive.

"Talk to me," I said.

"Can you handle big?" he asked me.

"Big?" I replied contemptuously. "I eat big for breakfast."

A small smile creased his lips, like the swale in the fairway at sixteen at Glen Abbey. "I like your style," he said.

"All part of the job," I said, acting as cool as the guy at Fenton's who discovers the waiter left the desserts off the bill.

"I'm talking about a killing," the big stranger said softly.

"Uh-huh," I responded, trying to keep my right eyebrow from flying up the front of my head like a Jesse Barfield pop-up.

"I'm talking quick and clean," he went on.

"Sure," I said, as unflappable as a Roy Thomson Hall bartender.

"And I'm talking sure thing."

"Sure thing?" I replied. "Now, you know —"

He cut in like a rush hour cab driver. "I'm also talking seven figures."

I was like a moving van in the Gardiner Expressway fast lane; he wasn't getting past me that easily. "Is that with or without the decimal point?" I asked.

"Without," he said curtly.

I did some quick mental arithmetic. Seven figures *without* the decimal point, that was six zeroes, so two commas . . . John Graves Simcoe's ghost! The man was talking megabucks. If this went through, that condo in Florida was mine for the taking. I could maybe even upgrade my Argo season tickets. Beads of sweat erupted on my brow like the condensation on the side of an Molson Export tallboy. "No problem," I said. "Quick clean killing, sure thing, seven figures. Piece of cake."

"Good," he said smiling like Harold Ballard at a full house. He extended his hand; it was the size of a Shopsy's corned beef sandwich, in the old days. "So you can handle this little job for me?"

"Are you kidding?" I could feel confidence returning, surging through me like the King Street car gathering speed west of Bathurst. "Hell, mister, I'm a stockbroker!"

SATURDAY LITE

75 cents

Playing Loto 6/49.
Chances only
slightly decreased
for those not par-
ticipating, experts
say

Is this man
the next Prime
Minister?
Donald Sutherland
reveals all

Exclusive photos
of the Ottawa
Press Club's
Annual Wet Brain
Contest.

SATURDAY LITE MAGAZINE

At last, *Saturday Night* is able to bring to the provinces its intellectually-reduced spin-off, *Saturday Lite*. In our première issue — guaranteed to become a collector's item — you can discover:

- the truth behind Richard Hatfield

- Is Government spending out of control? Mila Mulroney's personal account

- Saskatchewan's Grant Devine reveals his culinary delights. Simply Devine!

- Plus much, much more!

SATURDAY LITE — OPIUM FOR THE MASSES
WE DELIVER!

Yes, rush me my opium now

Name _____

Address _____

_____

SUBSCRIBE NOW and receive this fabulous BONUS: life-size poster of Robert Fulford

Who Has Had The Wind?

Starring Michael J. Fox

W. O. Mitchell's gripping tale of the troubled boyhood of Tommy Douglas, and his desperate attempt to form the NDP.

Never Cry Wolfe

Featuring Michael J. Fox in Wolfe's clothing

Farley Mowat's unusual adaptation of the battle for Quebec City. Bruno Gerussi guests as the French general, Montcalme.

Dance of the Happy Shades
Animated

Cartoon version of Alice Munro's touching story of a pair of cheap sunglasses that wanted to join The Winnipeg Ballet.

WC Super Channel

Complete Guide to TV Listings

M.A.S.H.
Canadian Content Version
The zany exploits of a group
of P.E.I. potato farmers.

This Hour Has Seven Days
The quintessential CBC
show.

Webster
A gruff Scottish broadcaster,
living in Vancouver, adopts
an orphaned easterner and
hilarity results in their
cultural conflicts.

The Beach Cronies
In this episode Constable
John falls down and hurts
himself, Nick has a shave,
and Derelict forgets to wash.
(Repeat)

Empire Inc. Strikes Back
Mini-series
The story continues; more
sex, more wealth, and more
episodes planned for the
future.

The Crosbie Show
The trials and tribulations of
a prominent Newfoundland
family.

Mommie Dearest
Movie
The story is based on a
former Prime Minister's
psychic communications with
his deceased mother.

Let's Make a Deal
Videotaped highlights of the
Canada/U.S. Free Trade
negotiations.

All in the Family
Situation Comedy
A group of zany Montréal
gangsters settle accounts
without interference from
the local police.

Haggle Rock
U.S. puppets make a ludicrous
land claim on Canadian
wildlife preserve, Machias Seal
Island, just off the coast of New
Brunswick.

Cole Porter's Ode to Canada

You're Canuck! You're the arctic tundra,
You're Canuck! You're a Joe Clark blundra,
You're a Socred fan of a Premier Vander Zalm,
You're a B.C. sawyer, a Bay Street lawyer, you're
                                        Canadarm!

You're high-tech, you're the Calg'ry Herald,
You're the wreck of the Ed Fitzgerald,
You're Liona strumming a Burton Cummings tune,
You're the Forum's timer, you're Moses Znaimer, you're
                                        Norm Bethune!

You're the mood of a St. John's shower,
You're the food at the CN Tower,
I'm a Brit, a Jap, a Wop, a Lapp, a Schmuck!
But if I'm a rank outsider, you're Canuck!

You're Canuck! You're a prairie oyster,
You're a yuck told by Wayne and Shoister,
You're a Dave Stieb blister, the Dionne sisters' mum,
You're Gary Nylund, you're Baffin Island, you're
Barbara Frum!

You're the bore on the Bay of Fundy,
You're the snore of Vancouver's Sunday,
You're Gouzenko blabbing, the Mounties nabbing their
guy,
You're an ice-cold Molson, you're Clifford Olsen, you're
Northrop Frye!

You're the rush of Niagara's torrents,
You're the mush of a Margaret Laurence,
You're a CN cargo, a T.O. Argo play,
You're an eastern mallard, you're Harold Ballard, you're
Jeanne Sauvé!

You're the swat of a Barfield homer,
You're the plot of a Richard Rohmer,
I'm a chink, a wog, a foreign dog, worse luck!
But if I'm a worthless Yankee, you're Canuck!

WAYNE & SHUSTER
— comedians.

1867 and All That
The Roots of Canadian Angst

1670
A Bad Start

The Hudson's Bay Company was established, and the Canadian fashion industry still hasn't recovered.

1690
Making it in the States

Pierre le Moyne, sieur d'Iberville, overran Newfoundland and Acadia. After this Canadian success, he left for greater stardom in the USA by overrunning Louisiana, thus setting a precedent by which all subsequent Canadians have been bound.

1738
An Unspeakable Discovery

Pierre Gauthier de Varennes obtained a licence to trade in Canada on condition he found a route through the Rockies to the western sea. Instead, he found Saskatchewan, for which his license was revoked as punishment. News of his appalling discovery was suppressed until 1905.

1859
A Canadian Prodigy

Known as The Golden Age of the Atlantic region. Nova Scotia reached its economic peak.

1867
The Start of Something Big

The separate colonies of British North America joined in a federal union to form the Dominion of Canada. This date marks the beginning of collective Canadian angst, as opposed to earlier isolated incidents.

1870
Trouble in Red River Country

Louis Riel, tired of being just another over-educated Métis, organized a council of war, seized Fort Garry, and forced Canada to create the province of Manitoba. For this he was driven into exile. Unfortunately, Riel failed where Pierre le Moyne had succeeded, and returned to Manitoba declaring that he would rather be executed than live in the USA.

1873
The Transcontinental

Prime Ministers Macdonald and Mackenzie promised B.C. a railroad, but later confessed that "the transcontinental" was just a new dance during which you seduced westerners while stepping on their toes.

1903
The Bitterness of Betrayal

Canada suffered a humiliating defeat when Britain ceded a large portion of British Columbia to the United States in settlement of the Alaskan boundary dispute. This event gave rise to the Canadian game of "Monkey in the Middle."

1905
The Age of Teetolatitarianism

Alberta and Saskatchewan joined Canada, and immediately initiated an era of rampant temperance and celibacy, from which they never quite recovered. They are still held responsible for Canada's deep-rooted feelings of guilt and angst.

1931
The New Canadians

The statute of Westminster gave legal effect to the idea that Canada was equal in status with Britain. This allowed all Canadians independant access to snobbery, poverty and ill-feelings towards the French. A right to their own humour, however, was not part of the bargain.

1949
The Last Straw

Newfoundland joined confederation.

1963-4
The Two Solitudes

The Pearson government appointed a royal commission on bilingualism and biculturalism. The controversial result was the production of a new Canadian flag showing two angry men with a vertical red bar on each side.

1984
Futilitarianism
A New Concept

Brian Mulroney, having hypnotized an unsuspecting electorate, swept to power. A traumatized nation is forced to relive the Diefenbaker era.

**The Pope
experiences Angst
after a recent
tour of Canada.**

The Top Ten Questions Most Troubling Canadians

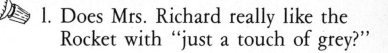

1. Does Mrs. Richard really like the Rocket with "just a touch of grey?"

2. Can Tommy Hunter's face really hold a day's rain?

3. Are the brothers of "the Fathers of Confederation," the uncles?

4. Does Canada have a Moral Majority, or just the NDP?

5. Is the "provincial tree" of British Columbia a stump?

6. If cured ham goes for $7.95 per pound, what does that make John Crosbie worth?

7. CENSORED CENSORED Ontario Censor Board CENSORED or not?

8. If Al Waxman is the "King of Kensington," who's the Queen? Toller Cranston?

9. Is Jean Drapeau's first name Mayor?

10. How 'bout those Blue Jays?

Things the Encyclopedia of Canada Left Out

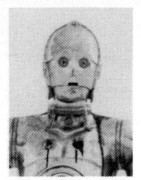

Marcel Mangegateau

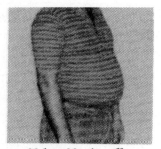

a Molson Muscle sufferer

the P.E.I. Film Board building

MANGEGATEAU, Marcel Born Sherbrooke, Quebec, in 1940. Canadian Forces Master Sergeant originally selected to be the first Canadian in space as part of the NASA Space Shuttle Program. Was rejected at the last minute when he refused to chip in for his share of the gas.
See also: *Token, Garneau Marc*

CHIPPY Adjective, as in "chippy play". Laudable physically aggressive play in the game of ice hockey.
See also: *Manslaughter*

NEWFIE JOKE A humourous anecdote about the means, manners and morays of the inhabitants of Newfoundland province. As in "How many Newfies does it take to screw in a lightbulb?" Fifty. One to hold the bulb and forty-nine to turn the room.

NATOOK A disk of bannock bread left to harden three months in the sun. The Alberta Crow Indian equivalent of the American-originated 'frisbee' flying disk.

MOLSON MUSCLE Protuberant fleshy abdomen obtained by drinking the beverages of the Molson Brewing Co. Ltd.
See also: *Brewer's Droop*

THE P.E.I. FILM BOARD A little known regional offshoot of the National Film Board. Federally funded, this group funds film endeavors pertaining to the history, cultivation, marketing and consuming of potatoes and potato products.

A FROOZE A group of two or more snowmen. As in a 'pride' of lions, a 'gaggle' of geese, a 'pod' of whales, etc. A frooze of snowmen.

Sir Edward Trans-Canada

CANADIENS

Greater Nanaimo
Crested Woodpecker

COLON, Ontario A small (population: 4500) Northern Ontario community of note for being the first municipality to be the site for both a toxic waste dump AND a nuclear generating station. Recently it has gained national notoriety by boasting a 100% employment rate, including children. The town's population lease themselves out to neighbouring communities as nightlights.

TRANS-CANADA, Sir Edward 1810-1879 Born in Sno-cone, Ontario. Canada's first Minister of Transport in the government of Sir John A. MacDonald. Served in Parliament 1867-1875. Canada's longest highway was named in his honour in 1948.

NEWBRUNSQUIK A popular hot beverage in Eastern Canada. Made of hot cod milk and dark Acadian chocolate.

MONTREAL CANADIENS HOCKEY CLUB EMBLEM This well known emblem was adopted in 1924 and has been worn by the club's players ever since. It was taken from the painted inscription in the middle of the rink at the old Montreal Forum — CH (Center Hice).

THE GREATER NANAIMO CRESTED WOODPECKER Inhabitant (formerly) of the coastal forests of British Columbia and the Gulf Islands. This once populous indigenous bird is now extinct in Canada. When British Columbia began exporting raw logs to Japan in the late 1970s these hardy birds began migrating to the Japanese islands with the log ships. The last crested woodpecker left Canada's shores in July 1985. The last tree is expected to follow in 1988.

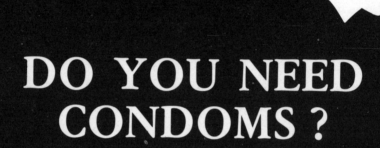

DO YOU NEED CONDOMS ?

NO SURPRISES !

For intercourse with the least results use **CANADIAN SHIELD**

Available in the Canadiana section at a pharmacy near you

Sex Education 101

If you're ready, class, we'll begin. Childish snickering is not at all helpful to the learning process, Smithers. Thank you. We haven't an awful lot of time, as you know. "Sex and Canadians" is merely a half course.

To begin with, there are those who will argue that sex and Canadians are incompatible, that the phrase "sex and Canadians" is an oxymoron. Do you all know what an oxymoron is? Yes, Dobrowolski, military intelligence is the most famous example. Very good. Indeed, Progressive Conservative is another. What was that, Smithers? Sober consideration? Ha ha!

Now, there is a theory that sex simply did not happen in this country prior to the 1960s, and that the population was maintained entirely through immigration. What do you make of this theory? Not so, I'm afraid. You must remember that for much of Canada's early history, a large percentage of the population was French, and we know what they're like. Well, if you don't know, it's certainly not for me to tell you.

However, modern historians, working from contemporary documents, now conclude that there were isolated outbreaks of sex among English-speaking Canadians as early as the late eighteenth century, even in Toronto. You needn't look so surprised, Smithers. And no, I mean sex between men and women. Simultaneously. No, Smithers, that is a misconception. Not all Torontonians are . . . . No, we don't say that anymore, Smithers; we say gay. Anyway, no they're not all gay in Toronto. I've been there myself.

In any case, there is little recorded evidence of sex in Canada. We do not associate William Lyon Mackenzie King or Louis St.

Laurent, for instance, with sexual activity. Sex in the 1950s was almost entirely restricted to Irving Layton, and he may just have been boasting.

Now, can anyone tell me who brought sex to Canada? No, Dobrowolski, it was not Arthur Hailey. Nor was it Joey Smallwood. No answers? Goodness, were you all born yesterday? Very well, then, sex was brought to Canada by Gerda Munsinger in 1961. I doubt very much that her name was on the tip of your tongue, Smithers, and if that was meant as a joke I'm afraid it misfired.

Gerda Munsinger was what was known at the time as a "blonde bombshell." She was an East German sexpot. Very good, Smithers, that is indeed another example of an oxymoron. Gerda Munsinger cut a swath through the Diefenbaker Cabinet, which was probably neither very difficult nor particularly pleasant. It was most likely the unpleasantness of the task as much as Ms. Munsinger's place of birth that provoked allegations that she was a spy. She admitted to hanky-panky — as sexual activity was called at that time — but not to spying, a story that has never quite rung true. It is interesting that the alleged canoodling — another term for sex in that era — took place in 1961, but no one noticed until March, 1966. This is not unusual for sexual activity between a German and a Canadian.

A unique flurry of sexual behaviour coincided with large-scale immigration from Italy. What the Italians brought to Canada was pasta, home-made wine, and sex. During the sixties, the Italians were very high profile, sex-wise. They made a lot of movies with busty, pouting actresses in exaggerated underwear. There was much physical activity that suggested sex, but not much actual sex. In real life, young Italian men drove noisy cars, wore expensive shoes, and spent most of their time drinking coffee with other Italian men. They reproduced bountifully, however, so we can draw our own conclusions.

After the Italians came Pierre Trudeau, a man who dated Barbra Streisand, Margot Kidder, Anne Mortifee, and Liona Boyd, among many others. By this time, of course, everybody in Canada was having sex. The Prime Minister was merely leading the way.

For a time in the seventies, sex was all the rage. People all across Canada were having sex, even in Toronto. There were bars you could go to if you wanted to find someone to have sex with. Yes, even in Toronto. Of course, it was bound to end. Especially in Toronto. By the eighties, sex was finished. By that time, people had careers. In 1986 a federal cabinet minister had to resign simply for visiting a German strip club. Sex was tacky. Sex was uncool. It simply wasted time that could have been spent getting ahead. Sinclair Stevens knew this. You never heard about Sinclair Stevens having sex.

And so it goes. Canadians of our enlightened age keep fit, not to attract sexual partners, but to interest potential investors. And so it should be. Keep that in mind, Smithers.

That's all for this week, class. Next week: Sex in the 1990s — what we can do to prevent it.

True Canadian Romances

Gerda, Yuri and Pierre

There was romance in the air, but romance had always followed Gerda. Ottawa in 1959 was a city of romance, especially on this night of nights, with the fresh wintry wind swirling around the Peace Tower. Good to be alive in Ottawa in those days! John Diefenbaker had brought a new cosmopolitan air to this once provincial city, and a young German girl speeding through the snowy city streets in a taxi recalled her father's stories about pre-Great War Vienna. If you squinted a bit, you could imagine yourself in the Ringstrasse, particularly after you had taken a glass of champagne.

Tonight, Gerda had enjoyed two glasses of champagne while dressing, and it was a slightly tipsy heart that beat in her admirable breast. Not love again, she thought reproachfully. Gerda could always feel love before it struck. Once she had fought love. Then Yuri had convinced her not to fight, simply to let it happen. "You were made for love," Yuri had told her with that amusing Russian accent of his. And he made her feel that it was true. Yuri was unlike any man she had known before. They were usually so possessive.

But Yuri was different. He seemed almost to encourage Gerda to see other men. "You should get out more," he told her. His work — whatever it was — at the Soviet Embassy occupied many of Yuri's evenings, and he practically begged Gerda to take in the gay social whirl that characterized Ottawa in that golden age. Almost every night saw an embassy party or a glittering reception at the fascinating, old world Chateau Laurier. As Yuri pointed out so persuasively, this was her opportunity to mix with Canada's men of power. Why, at tonight's gala, she might meet cabinet ministers, if she were lucky!

The taxi stopped, and Gerda stepped out into the brisk night air. Her feeling that love was close at hand had grown stronger, and she scarcely felt the near-Arctic wind that swept off the canal. As she swept majestically into the Chateau Laurier ballroom she could sense eyes turning her way, but she looked straight ahead, until a familiar voice said, "Ah, there you are, Gerda."

It was the pleasant effeminate boy from the Prime Minister's Office. Gerda had forgotten his name, but he attended all the parties and he knew practically everyone, even Yuri. He took Gerda's arm and led her towards a well-groomed, Gallic-looking man who stood alone. In an instant she was face-to-face with a handsome, urbane French-Canadian. "Frau Munsinger," said the young aesthete, "The Honourable Monsieur Pierre Sévigny."

Gerda took a deep breath. A cabinet minister! She looked at the Associate Minister of National Defence, and gave him the demure, yet somehow saucy, look that had reduced many men to stammering fools. But Monsieur Sévigny was made of tougher stuff. Gallantly taking her hand, he pressed his firm lips gently to her soft skin, just below her exquisitely perfumed wrist, and whispered, "Enchanté, Frau Munsinger."

Gerda batted her eyes in that way she had — twice rapidly, once slowly. "You must call me Gerda," she said. "And you shall call me Pierre," he replied in his Gallic way. So love *had* been in the air, Gerda reflected. Yet even in her excitement, her reckless abandon, Gerda reminded herself that she must remember absolutely everything that happened that evening. Poor dear Yuri would be so full of questions . . .

Maggie and Mick

It was the best, the most wonderful night ever, thought Maggie as she skipped across the hotel room to the full-length mirror. She held the short pink summer dress up against her slim figure and frowned thoughtfully. It was a dress she loved, but was it grown-up enough? Tossing the dress carelessly on the back of a chair, she went back to the window and looked out. Lake Ontario glistened in the moonlight. "Golly," Maggie thought, "it's so romantic!"

She could hear music from down the hall, where the boys were staying. They would all be there at the party, Maggie told herself, feeling a shiver of excitement. She had just met the boys on this trip to Toronto! There were Bill and Charlie and Ron and Keith, and of course Mick. Maggie liked Mick the best of all.

Her hair still damp from the shower, Maggie moved away from the window to tackle once again the agonizing problem of what to wear. She slipped out of her bathrobe and put her dress on. Well, it certainly suited the bad girl image people were trying to give her. Maggie bit her lip. She knew what people were saying behind her back. They talked about her in Vancouver, they talked about her in Ottawa, now they were talking about her in Toronto. Well let them talk, she said to herself angrily. They weren't going to spoil her fun!

Maggie wondered if Pierre knew she had come to Toronto. She was supposed to be Pierre's girl. Lately, however, Pierre had been so stuffy, such an old fuddy-duddy. She didn't want to go steady with Pierre anymore, and she had given him his ring back. She was having fun now, dating other boys and playing with her new camera.

Maybe she should wear something casual, after all, Maggie thought. Jeans and a top, perhaps. Mick said it was just a little party, nothing fancy. After all, jeans did show off her cute bottom. Maggie sighed. Did Mick really like her? He was a sophisticated English boy, and he had dated an awful lot of girls. People said he had even gone "all the way" with some of them! This was a worrying thought. Would he expect anything like that from her?

She wrinkled her pretty little nose and changed into her jeans. If only she knew what the other girls would be wearing. She looked out the window and smoked one of the funny little cigarettes one of the boys had given her. It seemed to give her confidence. She wasn't going to worry about what people said, and she wasn't going to think about stuffy old Pierre and his silly old friends. She was going to the party with Mick, and her heart beat faster. It was a wonderful, wonderful night, and anything could happen . . .

Anne and Charles

There is no limit to what the love of a good woman can do for a man, Charles reflected as he looked out over his six hundred and forty acres of wheat. The scene was almost a clichéd view of life in the Canadian heartland, but for Charles it was his home and his livelihood. He had cause for satisfaction when he studied his fields of rippling Saskatchewan wheat. Anyone in Blumenhof could tell you that Charles had worked hard all his life and deserved everything he had.

And he had plenty. Oh maybe not by the standards of the folks who lived in the big cities, places like Regina and Winnipeg. The work of a wheat farmer meant little to them, though they were happy enough to eat their bread and their flapjacks. He wondered if his wheat would reach Toronto, wind up on the breakfast table of the woman he loved. Maybe that very morning Anne had started her day with shredded wheat from this very land. Did she ever think of him, he wondered?

He could understand why she wanted to live in Toronto. It was where showbusiness folk lived in this country. That's why she left her beloved Nova Scotia in the first place. It was funny to think of them — a wheat farmer from Saskatchewan and a singer from a Nova Scotia coal town, hopelessly in love.

But where could they live? Usually it was the woman's place to live where her man made his living, but Anne was an exceptional case. Anne was a star. Charles had been to Toronto to visit her; it was all right, Charles guessed, but it sure wasn't Saskatchewan. Still, for Anne he would go anywhere. But for the moment he kept a place for her in his Blumenhof home. He knew she would come to him soon. It was there in the words of her songs. He *had*, he knew, placed her on a pedestal. And it *was*, without question, so high a pedestal that surely she could see eternity. And where was eternity if not Saskatchewan; everyone said it was endless. And hadn't she said, years ago now, that if she could you know that she would fly away with him? Hadn't she even made the gesture of sending the Snowbirds flying in formation over his wheat farm, pointing him eastward? Charles sighed with satisfaction. The most beautiful, the most talented woman in Canada was his.

Maybe it was time to visit her again. The wheat could wait. If he left today, he could be in Toronto tonight. He wouldn't call first. He'd just surprise her. He could picture her face when she opened her door. He had been cruel to stay away so long . . .

Suzanne and Lenny

Suzanne sat alone, staring out her window but scarcely hearing the boats going by. The night had seemed to last forever, but now it was morning and he had gone. His name was Lenny, or something like that.

What a strange evening it had been. Suzanne had gone out for a meal with a couple of the other secretaries from the office. Afterwards, they had stopped in a bar, where she had met dark, quiet Lenny. He wasn't the kind of guy she usually went for, but there was an intensity to Lenny that she couldn't ignore. He said he was a poet. Suzanne had heard that line before.

They had a drink or two and Lenny read some of his poems to her. Suzanne found poetry a bit embarrassing and, after a couple of poems, she said, "Well, Lenny, don't give up your day job!" It was just a joke, but Lenny didn't laugh. It *was* his day job, he told her. Suzanne felt guilty after that, and pretended to take it more seriously.

They left the bar and went back to her place by the river, amid the garbage and the flowers. She wasn't sure why. Maybe she was lonely. Maybe she felt sorry for the guy. Whatever, she wished she'd done a little shopping. Lenny was hungry, and there had been almost nothing in the fridge. Finally she gave him some tea and a couple of oranges she had picked up at the little Chinese grocery store on the corner. Lenny obviously thought it a bit unusual. He had looked at her as if she was half crazy. He seemed to think the oranges themselves had come from China. Finally she gave up trying to explain.

He'd rambled on about some sailor he knew called Jesus. Was he bisexual maybe? It was certainly unusual to hear a Jewish guy like Lenny talking about Jesus. Still, she felt she could trust him somehow. After all, as Lenny himself had pointed out, he had touched her perfect body with his mind. Or was it the other way around?

Suzanne wondered if she'd see him again. Lenny didn't seem a one-night-stand kind of guy. After all, hadn't he told her that she'd got him on her wavelength? Hadn't he said he'd like to travel with her some time? That was promising. She furrowed her pretty brow as she looked out on the river. She tried to see the heroes he'd talked about, the ones in the seaweed. There were children in the morning, he had said. So what? In this neighbourhood there were always children in the morning, frequently leaning out of their windows.

Suzanne sighed. Was a poet really much of a catch? What was his last name? One of those Jewish names — Goldfarb or Greenspoon or Cohen, something like that. Her folks would go crazy. A Jewish poet! Suzanne sighed again. She wondered if Lenny would even remember her. Maybe he'd call some time . . .

Cathy and John

Cathy looked down at the sleeping figure of John. How like an angel he looked as he slept, innocent and vulnerable like a little boy. It was a side of John the public never saw.

Sometimes Cathy thought she should have been a nurse. She seemed to have spent half her life taking care of people. Men, of course. Comforting them, cleaning up after them, yes even giving them their injections when necessary. But the life of a nurse would not have satisfied Cathy. She needed to get around, meet people, be at the centre of things. Certainly she had managed that in her thirty-five years.

Her life in the music business, her closeness to the stars, were not what she'd have known as a nurse. She'd done pretty well, all things considered, for a girl from Burlington, Ontario. Not even Burlington. *Outside* Burlington, for Pete's sake.

Now here she was in L.A., staying with John at the Chateau Marmont. How long ago those heady days in Yorkville seemed. Sometimes, when Cathy looked in a mirror, she was surprised to see herself as she was now. Was this the fresh young face that had won all those hearts? Was the good life taking its toll after all these years? She could look good again. She could sing again. Maybe tomorrow she'd call around.

Later on she'd speak to John about it. John had connections in the music biz. Everybody liked John, and it was no bad thing in this town to be his girlfriend. John's girlfriend! It was a dream come true. Maybe it was time she settled down. She and John had never discussed the future, but maybe someday she might even be — dare she say it — Mrs. John Belushi!

John was fast asleep. Maybe later on, when he woke up, she would talk to him about everything. Cathy looked at John, lying silently beside her. How sweet and peaceful he looked, how absolutely calm. If you didn't know better, you'd think he was barely breathing at all . . .

The Prince and Princess of Wales Unofficial Royal Tour Scrapbook

Beginner's Guide has managed to obtain the following exclusive photos from the Prince and Princess's private collection. These pictures are published here for the first time.

First stop, Vancouver

Chuck and Di stop to chat with another well-known visitor to Expo

The B.C. Interior

The wacky royals took time out
from their busy official schedule
to frolic in the cool waters of
Harrison Lake.

After a brief visit to Calgary for a spot of shopping, the royal couple roughed it on an Indian reservation in Manitoba.

Downtown Calgary

With the Blackfoot Indians

Visiting a Canadian Wildlife Compound

A brave Princess Di
joined her husband
at the London, Ontario,
game farm, but they were
soon on their way to
scenic Pointe Claire, Quebec,
on the banks of the
mighty St. Lawrence River.

On Montreal's West Islar

The Ménagerie à Trois

by John Williams

(Canadian protégé of Tennessee Williams)

ACT ONE

SCENE ONE

The scene is a rustic interior, somewhere in Canada. It could be Newfoundland or Saskatchewan or any damn place like that. It sure as hell isn't some luxury condo in Toronto, that's for sure. All the men are called John and all the women Debbie. As the curtain rises — what am I saying? Canadian theatres don't have curtains. As the lights go up, Debbie (the mother), played by Barbara Hamilton, is sitting knitting. Debbie (the older daughter), played by Margot Kidder, is sitting doing her nails, dressed in the slinkiest dress in the Eaton's catalogue. Debbie (the younger daughter), played by Megan Follows, is sitting at a table, doing her homework. John (the younger son), played by Saul Rubinek, is at a coffee table, performing an act of taxidermy on a dead duck.

Debbie (the mother): For Pete's sake, Debbie, leave them nails alone. You'll worry them to death.
Debbie (1st daughter): Aw Mom, don't get on my case.
Debbie (the mother): And don't talk back neither. Sometimes you sound like something out of "The Beachcombers."
Debbie (2nd daughter): Is it true John's coming home today?

Debbie (the mother): Well, that's what he said in his letter, isn't it?

Debbie (2nd daughter): I guess so. But why?

Debbie (the mother): Well, I don't know, do I? He doesn't tell me nothing.

Debbie (2nd daughter): Maybe he's found a girl. Maybe he's bringing her back here to meet us.

Debbie (1st daughter) (Looks up sharply): You don't know what you're talking about!

Debbie (2nd daughter): Oh yeah?

Debbie (1st daughter): Yeah!

Debbie (the mother): Now quit that, you two. You'll wake your father.

John (the father) (Offstage): Debbie!!

Debbie (the mother): Now look what you've done.

Debbie (2nd daughter): I looked in the case. There's only two bottles left.

Debbie (the mother): In that whole case? He only got it on Tuesday.

Debbie (2nd daughter): That's twenty-two bottles of Golden, at three hundred and forty-one millilitres a bottle, that's —

Debbie (the mother): Never you mind! Your father's a good man.

Debbie (1st daughter): Ha!

Debbie (the mother): You button your lip, young lady.

Debbie (1st daughter): You think I don't notice the way he stares at me?

Debbie (2nd daughter): Everbody stares at you. They say you're a whoo-er.

Debbie (1st daughter): A what?

Debbie (2nd daughter): A whoo-er.

Debbie (1st daughter): That shows how much you know. It's whore. Not whoo-er.

Debbie (2nd daughter): Well, I guess you should know anyhow.

Her sister starts up toward her, but is interrupted.

John (the father) (Offstage still): Debbie!! Where's my damn teeth?

Debbie (1st daughter): Someday I'm going to get out of here.

Debbie (the mother): They're under the damn bed.

Debbie (1st daughter): I'll go to Saskatoon. Maybe even Regina.

Debbie (2nd daughter): Why don't you go all the way to Winnipeg while you're at it?

Debbie (1st daughter): Maybe I will at that!

Debbie (2nd daughter): Ha! Winnipeg'd swallow you up.

Debbie (1st daughter): Shows what you know. Maybe I'll go and stay with John.

Debbie (2nd daughter): Sure, John's going to like having his sister living with him. That's very believable.

Debbie (1st daughter): Oh, what do you know anyway?

Enter John, the father, known as Big John. There is a ripple of applause. Few members of the audience have seen Lorne Greene live before.

Big John: What the hell were my teeth doing under the bed?

Debbie (the mother): Dog was playing with them last night.

Big John: Damn. Thought they tasted funny.

Debbie (the mother): Jeez, Big John, can't you put a decent shirt on?

Big John: What in hell for?

Debbie (the mother): John's coming home today.

Big John: Aw hell. That boy's as useless as "The Journal."

Debbie (the mother): Now don't say that, Big John.

Big John: He's as useless as a Swedish defenceman.

Debbie (the mother): Be gentle with the boy, John.

Big John: The boy's as useless as Pierre Berton's sideburns.

Debbie (the mother): You're still mad he went to work for the CBC.

Big John: You bet I'm mad. All right for him. He lives in Winnipeg. I gotta stay here and take the flak. I go into town for some feed, the fellas give me one hell of a time.

Debbie (the mother): I know. But he's only an accountant at the CBC. It's not as if he's really *in* the CBC.

Big John: What was wrong with insurance? He was happy in insurance. I was proud of him.

Debbie (the mother): I remember.

Big John: Then he came back here a year ago.

Debbie (the mother): I remember.

Debbie (the mother): The sky was a dappled grey. The sun came through in slivers, like through the slat plank walls of an old barn.

Debbie (the mother): And in the late afternoon, there were little soft pink clouds, like the bums of little boys.

Big John: I remember.

Debbie (the mother): I remember.

Big John: And he sat in that chair and said, "Dad, I've quit the insurance company. I've gone to the CBC."

Debbie (the mother): I didn't know the CBC even had an office in Winnipeg.

Big John: It was the worst day of my life.

Debbie (the mother): He told me the CBC has offices all over Canada.

Big John: I wanted to kill him.

Debbie (the mother): Offices and studios.

Big John: He sat in that chair.

Debbie (the mother): Both radio and television.

Big John: He'd never called me Dad before.

Debbie (the mother): The sky was a dappled grey.

Debbie (1st daughter): I could be happy in Winnipeg.

Debbie (the mother): There were clouds like little boys' bums.

Debbie (1st daughter): I could stand at the corner of Portage and Main.

Big John: I said, "What do you mean, the CBC?"

Debbie (1st daughter): I've never known happiness.

Debbie (2nd daughter): Someday I'll finish my homework.

Big John: I could have killed the little son of a bitch.

John (2nd son) (Looking up from his duck): What's everyone talking about?

Just before the audience leaves in despair, the door opens. In steps John, the older son, played by R.H. Thomson. With him is Debbie (a stranger), played by Jackie Burroughs. The family looks on in silence.

John (1st son): Hi Mom, Dad, Debbie, Debbie, John. I'd like you to meet Debbie. Debbie, Mom, Debbie, Dad, Debbie, Debbie, Debbie, Debbie, Debbie, John. Everybody, this is Debbie.

Debbie (the stranger): Hi!

Debbie (1st daughter): Holy mother of God!

Debbie (2nd daughter): She sure is skinny!

Debbie (the mother): At least her name's Debbie.

Big John: It's a woman!

Debbie (the mother): Well, of course it's a woman, you great cowflap!

Big John: Well, I just thought —

Debbie (the mother): What did you think, you damn fool?

Big John: Well, working for the CBC and all —

John (1st son): Debbie and I have something to tell you.

Debbie (1st daughter): Oh sweet Jesus no!

John (1st son): I've been transferred to Toronto.

Big John: Mother of Christ!

John (1st son): Debbie and I are going together. We met at an office party. We've got a condo in Flemingdon Park.

Debbie (the mother): Flemingdon Park! Sweet Jesus!

Big John: It's a woman, for God's sake. I thought he was —

Debbie (2nd daughter): Gay?

Debbie (1st daughter): Gay? John? You can't be serious. John and I have been lovers since I was twelve!

Debbie (the stranger): Oh my God!

Debbie (1st daughter): He's the only man I've ever loved!

John (1st son): Debbie!

Debbie (the stranger): John!

Debbie (1st daughter): John!

Big John: Debbie!

John (2nd son): John? Gay? Listen, I'm the one who's gay!

Debbie (the mother): Gay? John?

Big John: Gay? I thought he was just quiet!

Debbie (the mother): You damned old alcoholic!

Big John: Alcoholic? I'm not an alcoholic?

Debbie (the mother): Then who's been drinking all that beer then?

Debbie (2nd daughter): I have. I'm the alcoholic.

Big John: You? You've been drinking my Golden?

Debbie (the mother): There's only two bottles left.

Big John: Two bottles! Sweet Jesus, I only bought that case on Tuesday!

Debbie (2nd daughter): It's the pressure of school.

John (1st son): Mother of God!

Debbie (2nd daughter): At first it was just one bottle, to get me through my homework. Then it was two. Now it's out of control.

John (2nd son): Nobody's listening to me! I'm gay, I tell you!

Debbie (1st daughter): I love my brother!

Debbie (2nd daughter): Sometimes I even drink rye!

Debbie (1st daughter): He seduced me when I was twelve. He was fourteen. He'd been playing hockey. There was still the sweet damp smell of sweat on him. He told me he loved me.

John (2nd son): Do you hear me? I'm gay! I'm as queer as Saskatchewan's drinking laws.

Debbie (2nd daughter): I have a couple of beers at lunchtime.

Big John: Great flying angels of mercy!

Debbie (the mother) (To Debbie the stranger): Come in, dear. Wipe the snow off your feet. Take your parka off.

Debbie (the stranger): Thank you, Mrs —

Debbie (the mother): Oh, call me Debbie. Everybody does.

Debbie (the stranger): Well, Debbie, you have a lovely home!

Black out

BEATON'S*
PREVIEW
fall
A Supplement

99% OFF!
BEATON'S ENTIRE
WINTER COAT
SELECTION!

* Also available in Québec
without the apostrophe 's'.

BEATON'S own Vanity Wear Exclusives!

A. Saskatchewan pajamas made of fibre-dyed, deglutenated wheat. Choice of colours — prints or solids. Sizes S, M, L, XL, XXL, XXXL
Each **62**⁹⁹

B. A nightie-night gown with an easy-to-trip-over hem. Choice of colours. Sizes S, M, L, XL, XXL, XXXL
Each **64**⁹⁹

C. A blend of scratchy fibres, this robe is a must-have for those cold winter nights. Its deep pockets are handy for storing those slightly used tissues needed for bouts with Canadian colds. No colour choice. One colour fits all.
Each **89**⁹⁹

50%

off our
Tender Touch
living bras.

A. "Thank GOD it fits!"
Unmoulded stretch bra
for the trés, trés, petite
figure. Assorted colours.
One size fits all.

B. The "Ultra, Ultra"
24-Hour Fibrefill Bra.
Ultra-padded, ultra-
comfort, ultra-priced.
Assorted sizes.

C. All leather Cross-Your-
Heart biker's bra.
Lightly lined for soft,
cool comfort with lace
trim.

D. "OOPS" Wunderbra! So
soft, so sheer, so com-
fortable, it's . . . like
wearing nothing at all.
Assorted sizes.

E. The Taut-Tummy-Plus
control-top with extra
thick wood panel. Vinyl-
lined to prevent
splinters. Maximum
discomfort.

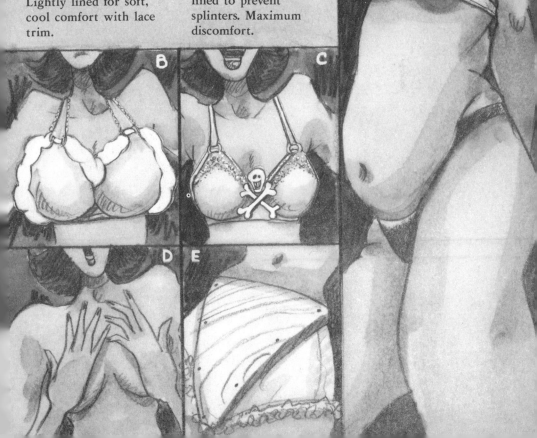

Absolutely NOTHING OFF!
Famous BEATON brand crumpled sweaters.

Each 1⁹⁹

Beaton's Institute for the Bland brings you our new mix'n'match line of drab sweaters.

A. Crew neck pullover. Available in assorted light grey colours.
B. No-neck pullover. Available in assorted dark grey colours for that pass-me-by look. Sizes S, M, L, XL, and don't even ask!

FIRST AID

A benefit concert for the over-privileged first world

Toronto, April 1st,
Maple Leaf Gardens

About the Band

Wayne Gretzky on accordian   René Lévèsque on the spoons
Don Getty on triangle   Larry Zolf, lead vocals
Featuring special guest Pope John Paul XXIII as rhythm ace

The First Annual Beginner's Guide Order of the Boot Award

The Order of the Boot is awarded to the producers of this postcard of Vancouver's night skyline, for ignorance above and beyond the call of provincial duty.

It seems that some easterner, possibly due to a misguided belief that no photo of British Columbia is complete without mountains, added some to the background.

A Beginner's Guide photo, taken during the day, clearly proves that this deception surely deserves The Order of the Boot.

Vancouver skyline as imagined by Easterners

Actual Vancouver skyline

Listen, You Can Hear the Sea!

1.

The Maritimes...

2.

Québec ...

O Ca - na - da   Our home and dum-dum land

True   dum-dum   love   in   all thy dum com - mand   With

O Dum-Dum Land

In a remarkable musical coincidence, the second act of *The Magic Flute* begins with the first four notes of "O Canada." After those four splendid notes, however, Mozart seems to lose his way a bit, never quite achieving the grandeur of Calixz Lavallée's theme.

Now, of course, we're all happy and proud to sing along with our National Anthem at the drop of a hat; unfortunately years ago the federal government changed the words. It's a known fact that nobody learns the words to a national anthem after the age of twelve, so those of us who had attained a greater maturity were effectively disenfranchised from our great Canadian paean.

The other obvious problem is the words we do know. Take "our home and native land." In a land of immigrants, "native" is inappropriate to many of us. Perhaps only our native people can sing that line with any confidence. The rest of us may feel reduced to singing "home and dum-dum land" — and woe betide us if we don't always feel entirely at home.

Those who agree with Dr. Johnson that patriotism is the last refuge of the scoundrel may encounter difficulties with "patriot-love," and feminists quite rightly fulminate about "thy sons command." Similarly, only a Canadian politician in power could sing "strong and free" with a straight face. Even if we allow "glorious," conscientious objectors may still decline to "stand on guard" without good reason.

So, taking out the bits that people find objectionable as well as the bits no one knows, we are left with this:

O Canada, our home and dum-dum land!
True dum-dum love in all thy dum command.
With glowing hearts we see thee rise,
The True North, dum and dum,
Dum-de dum dum dum, O Canada,
Dum dum dum dum-dum-dum for thee.
Dum dum de-dum, glorious and dum!
Dum dum de-dum, dum dum dum dum for thee,
O Canada, dum dum dum dum for thee!

This is clearly what has been referred to elsewhere as white scat-singing. Let's get with it! That sort of stuff was fine in 1880, but we've come a long way since then! Australia gave itself a new national anthem, so why not us? What we need is something that sounds stirring in a hockey arena and imposing at the National Arts Centre.

We've got plenty of good Canadian songs to choose from. "Sh-boom," a big hit for Toronto's Crewcuts back in the fifties, is a bright, up-tempo piece with the line, "Life could be a dream, sweetheart," which is a Canadian sentiment if there ever was one. The recurring line "Ya-da-da-da-da-da-da-da-da-da-da" could be sung derisively at visiting teams before hockey games to great effect, though it might be felt a little informal for state occasions.

All right, if you want something a little more sedate, try Leonard Cohen's "Suzanne" on for size. It's solemn enough, God knows, although it's difficult to picture a crowd of fifty thousand singing "He's touched your perfect body with his mind" prior to an Expo game. Neil Young's "Helpless" might be appropriate before an international hockey game, albeit a trifle defeatist. On the other hand, Parachute Club's "Rise Up" could be considered a little inflammatory during Royal tours. "Farewell to Nova Scotia" is an oft-expressed Canadian feeling, but it's unacceptably regional, as is "Sudbury Saturday Night" by Stompin' Tom Connors. Anne Murray's "Snowbird" would win a lot of admirers, but its suggestion of mass emigration might disqualify it (unfairly) as an expression of national aspiration. "Four Strong Winds," and "Early Morning Rain," all capture our unique climate but give us little cause for pride.

There is one song, written by a Canadian, admittedly for an American, that could unite us all. There is one song that typifies our national ruggedness and disdain for the world's opinion. It could ring through our sports halls and throw fear into Russian hockey stars and the New York Yankees alike, or set international summit conferences into a state of trembling respect. We refer, of course, to that masterwork of Ottawa's own Paul Anka, "My Way." Look what it did for Sinatra. It could do as much, and more, for us. Think about it. Imagine a sell-out crowd at B.C. Place singing as one, "I chewed it up and spit it out." Awesome. Beat the rugged individualist Americans at their own game. Let's see the Yankees come on like world-beaters after a full house of Blue Jay fans belt out, "I Did It My-y-y-y-y-y-y-y-y-y W-a-a-a-a-a-a-y-y-y!"

Let's do it! Let's sing out! Let's put this country on the map!

Paul Schaffer
Born in Thunder Bay

**Paul Schaffer's new album pays tribute
to his Canadian roots**

SIGN LANGUAGE
An Addendum for the Walkman Impaired

For decades, those with hearing and speech handicaps have been able to communicate using the *language* of hands; a complex dialogue of signals and gestures each communicating a letter, word or phrase. Sadly, despite the increasing quantity and complexity of communication demanded by modern society a growing sector of our population is losing its communications skills altogether — The Walkman Impaired. For these unfortunates we offer this addition to the international hand signals for the deaf. A modern addendum of the hand signal language designed specifically to cope with their specific communication demands.

International Hand Symbols for the Deaf

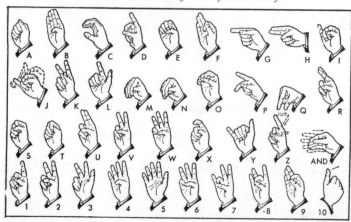

How's your reception?

Static

Manilow

My batteries are low

Political broadcast

I'm from Vancouver

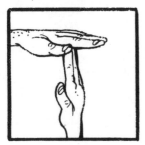

I'm from Toronto

I'm from the Maritimes

I'm from Quebec

Got any cigarettes?

Got any Preparation H?

So long, sucker

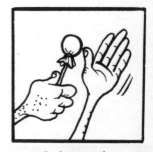

Let's go to McDonalds

Need any life insurance?

Have you seen my llama?

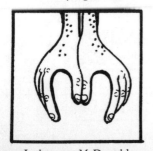

New Canadian Bills

The Princess Di Dollar Bill

The Mulroney "2"

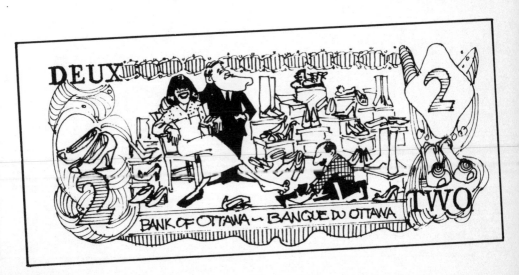

The "Labatt 50"

Bill 101

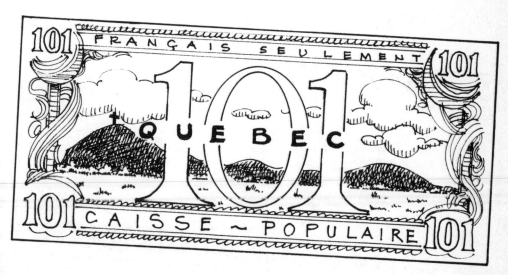

· CANADIAN
INQUIRER

Beginners's Guide Special

★★★ **World Exclusive** ★★★

PARTY ANIMAL RICHARD HATFIELD IS FRISKED AT LOCAL SENIORS CENTRE

CANADIAN INQUIRER EXCLUSIVE

BURTON CUMMINGS' PASSIONATE NEW NATIONAL ANTHEM

EXCLUSIVE STORY INSIDE

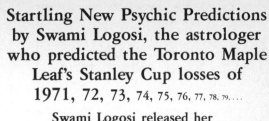

Startling New Psychic Predictions by Swami Logosi, the astrologer who predicted the Toronto Maple Leaf's Stanley Cup losses of 1971, 72, 73, 74, 75, 76, 77, 78, 79....

Swami Logosi released her predictions for the next twelve months today. Among her amazing predictions, Logosi, well-known for her chilling accuracy, foresees:

Brian Mulroney will have a run of bad luck. His popularity will slump in the polls and he'll develop sinus problems; he'll begin to sound more and more like an American.

Harold Ballard will convert to Communism! After a plane, on which he is a passenger, makes an emergency landing in Detroit, Ballard becomes a passionate believer in the communist system.

Toronto will strike Gold! Gold will be found in abundance in the windows of the Royal Bank building starting Canada's second biggest goldrush.

Famous Indian Princess Diawatha launches her line of Canadian cosmetics

Calgary — Princess "Di," at the gala launch of her new line of skin care products, claimed that they will revolutionize women's skincare.

Her new products contain an amazing recent discovery — TOTEM Jelly — an oil based substance containing medicinal properties found only in the Canadian tar sands.

Sold by the barrel, TOTEM is reasonably priced — at present. Diawatha cautioned, however, that prices might fluctuate depending upon world oil market conditions.

Princess Diawatha, a cosmetic industry magnate, recently celebrated her 58th Birthday by shooting an arrow through her head.

The
Ben Whips
Correspondence School of Art

Draw Binky!   **The Pirate!**   **The Pretty Girl!**

Everyone likes to draw. But **you** might have what it takes to go on to an interesting and rewarding career as a **professional artist**.

Take your time and draw one of the figures shown above, Binky the deer, the scowling Pirate or the Pretty Girl. Mr. Ben Whips has drawn these examples. Make your drawing any size except one that would look like a tracing.

Ben Whips will personally evaluate your work. You could even qualify as a candidate for the Ben Whips Correspondence School of Art.

Not everyone has what it takes to become a professional artist but **you** might. It's never too late to find out.

No obligation; free written analysis of your work. Send $17.95 to cover postage and handling. Don't delay.

THE BEN WHIPS CORRESPONDENCE SCHOOL OF ART

Dear Mr. Chiarosauro:

Crikey mate! Oi just received your drawing and it's bloody marvellous! I'm sending you an application form for my Ben Whips Correspondence School of Art straight away!

It just takes a little trainin', the right sort o' know-how that oi can provide -- a few lines here, a squiggle there, and 'Bob's yer Uncle', you've got bleedin' art! ''Cripes!'' you'll say, ''did oi do that?!'' And the next thing you know you'll get a noice leather brief-case, a handful of cab slips and you're a workin' artist, me ol' son! And you're on your way to a bleedin' ''Order of Canada'' if there's any justice.

There's a flippin' fortune to be made in art. I'm not kiddin' you! ''There's a flippin' fortune in the art game'' I was sayin' just the other day. To Princess Margaret.

So don't delay, return your completed application and cheque. You'll receive lesson one (Feet) and be on your way to a fulfilling career in professional art.

Yours,

Whips

Ben Whips

The Pirate by Mr. Roy Chiaroscuro
22 East Wheetigo
Regina, Saskatchewan

Semiology and the NHL
An Important Study

As everyone knows these days, semiology is the study of signs, or something like that. Philosophers, literary critics, and ad executives know all about it, and so should the rest of us.

Put briefly, we *are* what we call ourselves. In Canada we call our daughters Cathy and Debbie because we want our women-folk cute, pert, and unthreatening. Our sons are John and Michael because we want them vaguely masculine without being distinctive. Until the recent Yuppie Parent phenomenon, the last thing a Canadian parent wanted was a "distinctive" child — "distinctive" children being prey to practices like homosexuality, art, and other vices embarrassing to parents. In recent years we have taken to naming our children Kristin and Jason only because everyone else has done so, so it's perfectly safe.

This is perfectly rational behaviour in Canada, a country that boasts a pair of major maritime cities called St. John's and St. John, and a football team called the Roughriders and one called the Rough Riders. It takes a real Canadian to make these distinctions (test your friends).

What, then, can we learn from the logos of our NHL franchises? What are we telling ourselves about ourselves? Take the Toronto Maple Leafs, for instance. The Leafs present themselves with a plain blue maple leaf with the team name in the centre. Just a moment, you say. A *blue* maple leaf? Like the team's owner, the blue maple leaf does not occur in nature. Like the team's owner,

MAPLE LEAFS

the design has a pointed top, is fat in the middle, and has hardly a single foot on the ground. Although every leaf must fall, this one remains plump and indolent. It will be pressed between the pages of a Peter C. Newman first edition. The word sap comes readily to mind.

Canada's other long-standing team is Montreal's Canadiens.

CANADIENS

The Habs boast a lean corporate emblem that owes no allegiance to birds, beasts, native peoples, or any of the unlikely representations that characterize North American sports franchises. Their simple H within a C is a triumph of logo design, instantly recognizable and easy to read (unlike the Expo emblem, which could be anything at all and probably is). But what are the Canadiens telling us? Careening Hooligans? Husky Canucks? In the relative absence of francophones in recent teams, perhaps we should assume Canadiens Hinglish! Or perhaps the arrival of American players means Canada Huh? Semiologists are divided on this one.

Elsewhere in Quebec, the Nordiques have adopted a curious design that resembles nothing more than a platform shoe of the sort that was popular in the early-to-mid seventies, when Quebec nationalism was at its peak. This subliminal appeal to nationalist fervour has paid dividends for the anglophone brewery that owns the team. The platform shoe, of course, bears an uncanny

NORDIQUES

resemblance to the homely *sabot* worn by early Québecois, another factor in the team's popular success despite its reliance on Czech defectors.

Moving west, we come, all too soon, to the Winnipeg Jets. Do we associate jets with Winnipeg? Of course not, except in terms of getting out of town as quickly as possible. Perhaps we are meant to think of great Winnipeggers who have gone

JETS

elsewhere: Burton Cummings, Larry Zolf, David Steinberg, to name but a few. Perhaps this is Winnipeg's way of telling us that, although they don't actually expect to win anything themselves, they'd like to remind us that many of our greatest resources have flown out of their airport. Perhaps the stylized airplane in the logo is a reminder to locals of the route to the airport. Throughout the civilized world, motorists find airports by following exactly such signs. Go to Florida for the winter, it seems to say. Few leading semiologists make wagers favourable to the Winnipeg Jets.

And so to Alberta. The Edmonton Oilers have a spectacularly dull logo, displaying the word Oilers beneath what seems to be a drop of oil or perhaps a teardrop. This is appropriate for a team that owns the first dull superstar in the history of the game. An interview with Wayne Gretzky makes the Oiler logo look exciting. It is as stimulating as a

OILERS

Don Getty speech, and every bit as memorable. If you like *Klondike Days*, you'll love the Oilers' logo.

Further south in Calgary you get the Flames. A name steeped in Calgary history is that. The Calgary Flames are a fine example of that modern sports phenomenon, the sudden franchise shift. Some years ago, the Calgary Flames were the Atlanta

FLAMES

Flames. The team's logo captures the spirit of the move. Having been burned in Atlanta, the hockey boys fled under cover of night, the flames licking at their jerseys. When the team got the puck out of Atlanta, the good people of Calgary retained the name, hoping to trade on the rich heritage of Georgia hockey. Billy-Bob Geoffrion was a good ol' boy if ever there was one. It's not as funny as New Orleans Jazz moving to Salt Lake City and becoming Utah Jazz, but few things are.

Then there's Vancouver. Isn't there always? The Canucks are the team that, a few years ago, had their uniforms changed on the advice of a bright young fellow who thought their colours weren't intimidating enough. The team's record since then speaks for itself. The Canucks' logo speaks volumes. But what is it saying? A stylized skate (no commercial sponsorship here) hurtles downwards from right to left. Downwards? Is Vancouver's hockey rink built on the side of one of that city's mountains? Wouldn't all the ice accumulate at one end? And to the left? In a province that routinely hurtles towards the right? Is the emblem a subliminal attack on the NDP years in British Columbia? Are the Canucks an

CANUCKS

unwitting tool of the Socred government? Can they win under new head coach Bill "Cruncher" Vander Zalm? The semiologists say no. Not until they get that skate headed upward.

The 1985-86 NHL season bears out the semiologist's findings. The Canucks continued their downward progress, the Nordiques stumbled over their ungainly heels, the Oilers shed a dark, oily tear, and the Jets took off for a time but were forced to land. The sap-filled Leafs stayed on the tree longer than expected, but inevitably had to fall. The Flames were red-hot for a time but eventually burned themselves out. And at the end, who took all the glory for the umpteenth time? Who else but the representatives of Corporate Hockey?

- How many Wayne Gretzky's does it take to unscrew a lightbulb?
  — 18! (It's a team effort.)

- Why did Wayne Gretzky cross the road?
  —To get to his shopping mall.

- What's black & white & red all over? (and plays goal)
  — Grant Fuhr, Andy Moog and Vladislav Tretiak.

- Why is Edmonton Colliseum never hot?
  There's a fan in every seat.

- Texas Oil Millionaire "Why Kid, I'm so rich I could build a wall right around the state of Texas!"
  Wayne Gretzky "Why not do it; if I like it I'll buy it!"

LAFFS!

Who is TALLER? ★

Look carefully at the illustrations below; sometimes the eye can be deceived! Who has the greater stature, the two guys on the left, or Wayne Gretzky?

A. Eagleson
J. Ziegler

W.G

A. They are not even close to being the same...

Famous People Who Married Canadians

1. Suzanne Somers
2. Lynn Redgrave
3. Douglas Fairbanks and Buddy Rogers (same Canadian)
4. Carrie Snodgress
5. Tammy Grimes
6. George C. Scott
7. Alex Karras
8. Irving Thalberg
9. David Suskind
10. Eleanor Powell and Kathryn Hays (same Canadian)
11. Jacqueline Bisset
12. Peter Ustinov

Famous People Alleged to Have Had Sex With Canadians

1. Barbra Streisand
2. Dusty Springfield
3. Mick Jagger
4. Jane Fonda
5. Graham Nash
6. John Belushi
7. Jack Nicholson
8. Levon Helm
9. Hoyt Axton
10. Ron Wood
11. Richard Chamberlain
12. Groucho Marx
13. Peter Bogdanovich
14. Lou Rawls
15. David Letterman

Great Canadian Fighters

1. Tommy Burns
2. George Chuvalo
3. Shawn O'Sullivan
4. Willie de Wit
5. Whipper Billy Watson
6. Dave Schultz
7. Morley Callaghan
8. Sondra Gotlieb

Whatever Happened To . . . ?

1. René Simard
2. John Turner
3. Our Pet Juliette
4. Claude Charron
5. Margaret Trudeau
6. Paul Henderson
7. Frank Miller
8. Jack Horner
9. Charles Templeton
10. Nelson Skalbania
11. Peter Pocklington
12. Bachman-Turner Overdrive
13. Dave Stieb (Honorary Canadian)
14. Eugene Whelan

People Who Might As Well Have Been Canadians

1. George Hamilton
2. Jughead
3. Merv Griffin
4. Gerald Ford
5. Micky Dolenz
6. Steve Weed
7. Pope John Paul I
8. Judy Carne
9. Roger Whittaker
10. Pete Best
11. General Galtieri
12. Trini Lopez
13. Lumpy Rutherford
14. Zeppo and Gummo Marx
15. Paul and Paula
16. Rosencrantz and Guildenstern
17. The Chicago Cubs
18. George Bush
19. Mila Mulroney
20. Captain Scott of the Antarctic

Ten Dubious Canadians

1. Robert Goulet (b. Lawrence, Mass., lives California)
2. Arthur Hailey (b. Luton, England, lives Bahamas)
3. Brian Moore (b. Ireland, lives California)
4. Robert Service (b. Preston, England, d. Lancieux, France)
5. Malcolm Lowry (b. England, d. England)
6. Art Linkletter (b. Saskatchewan, left in infancy)
7. Glenn Ford (b. Quebec, left in infancy)
8. Saul Bellow (b. Quebec, ditto)
9. Gina Lollobrigida (b. Subiaco, Italy, nearly moved to Toronto in 1960)
10. Lord Stanley (b. England, d. England, donated Stanley Cup, never saw Canada)

The Ten Biggest Canadian Lies

1. The twentieth century belongs to Canada.
2. "It's hard not to think of The Bay."
3. Canada is not influenced by American foreign policy.
4. Urea formaldehyde insulation is completely safe.
5. We stand on guard for thee.
6. You can really enjoy winter if you just get out and make the most of it.
7. "When I come to Toronto, I come to play."
8. Free trade will benefit Canada.
9. The Canadian Charter of Rights.
10. I saw Gerda Munsinger only socially, maybe once or twice, and only at lunchtime.

The One Biggest Canadian Truth

Mon pays ce n'est pas un pays c'est l'hiver

Canadian Things We Cannot Explain to Ourselves

1. Why mosquitoes kill people in Winnipeg but nowhere else
2. Why so many Canadians are called Debbie
3. Why the CBC broadcasts so much curling when there are sports like lawn bowling, darts, and fly fishing available
4. Why we used to laugh at American beer but now we can't get enough of the stuff
5. Why, despite the international success of Alan Thicke and Alex Trebeck, we persist in not believing in ourselves
6. Why, given the amount of newspaper space and television time she gets, Carling Bassett never wins a tennis tournament
7. Why, in terms of being qualified to run the Stratford Festival, Robin Phillips and John Neville are considered Canadian, but John Dexter is not
8. Why there is an apostrophe in St. John's, Newfoundland
9. Why Montreal is the only place where drivers have to be told "attendez la feu verte"
10. Why Canada has the largest Doukhobor population in the world

Doukhobors settle on the prairies

Uncle Sam sucks eggs & ham

by Dr. Pseud

That Uncle Sam!
That Uncle Sam!
I do not like
That Uncle Sam!
I could not, would not buy his cars
Nor records, books, nor chocolate bars
I will not watch his movie shows
Nor will I wear the clothes he chose
I cannot stand his little wars
Those foreign wars are ALWAYS bores
I do not like his acid rain
I think his acid rain's insane
Nor do I like his national song
His bombing song, I think, is wrong
I do not like him here or there
I do not like him ANYWHERE
Not out in space! Not out at sea!
Not on dry land! You let us be!
I will not call him on the phone
I will not have him in my home
In fact I hope that Sam stays well
Below a certain parallel
I'd rather eat green eggs and ham
Than live this close to Uncle Sam!

We Can't Stand Americans

1. Because they come up here in the summer, wearing funny clothes and carrying skis on the tops of their station wagons

2. Because they never have anything but American money with them and they never change it at a bank and they complain about the exchange rate they get at stores

3. Because they refuse to vote for Blue Jay or Expo ballplayers on their All-Star Game ballots

4. Because of their tacky local newscasts in Buffalo and other crummy border towns

5. Because they elect judges and have stupid TV commercials for them

6. Because they're used to getting their booze almost for free and complain about our prices when they come here and we can't argue because they're right

7. Because their dollar is so high that it costs us a fortune to go down there for a few days and take advantage of their cheap booze

8. Because they don't know the first thing about Canada, like who our Prime Minister is — or even that we have a Prime Minister or a different currency. And they glaze over if we try to explain them

9. Because they don't even know that people like Lorne Greene, William Shatner, Rich Little, and Monty Hall are Canadians

10. Because the only time they pay attention to hockey is when they win something

11. Because they make terrible weak beer and spend so much money advertising it that every seventeen-year-old in the western world craves it

12. Because before Vietnam they used to claim they'd never lost a war even though we stuffed them in the War of 1812

13. Because they think Wayne Newton is a great entertainer

14. Because, although we're their leading trading partner and share the world's longest undefended border, they keep dropping cruise missiles on obscure bits of Alberta

15. Because they still haven't seen through Ron and Nancy, and they actually think that people like Teddy Kennedy are left-wing

Now staff, I advise you to keep your disguises on until they close the book.